Stay on the Bus

Navigating breast cancer, diagnosis, treatment
and those annoying people

Written by Andrea Moulding

Stay on the Bus

Navigating breast cancer, diagnosis, treatment
and those annoying people

Written by Andrea Moulding

First published in 2023

ISBN: 978-1-7391263-1-5

Published with the support of TAUK Publishing.

TAUK
Publishing

This book is dedicated to all my family. To Patrick and my children, who weathered the storms of diagnosis and treatment with humour. To my mum and her endless energy, support, and cleaning capabilities. Also, my sister Vanessa, for giving me the kick I needed to get this book finished. Special thanks must go to Isabelle and my brother Neil, who was a rock in many ways, not least for being a fabulous taxi driver and always keeping my spirits up through the hard times.

Get on the Bus!

Dear Reader

If you have picked up this book, you will have found yourself in a place that only happens to other people. Your head will be all over the place. That's normal and to be expected.

You will have experienced the usual pained faces and the hushed words too terrible to say out loud.

"Sorry to hear you have… cancer."

Please don't be too hard on them. Let's be honest, until your diagnosis, you were the same. People don't know how to react.

Get ready to receive the gifts. We don't mind the hand cream and luxury soaps, but you can keep *The Little Book of Hugs*. Be prepared for inspirational wall plaques and 'wisdom' quotes. Such as:

'It doesn't define you' and don't get me started on 'You have to fight it'.

Everyone is different, but for me, I was so busy crying, I only heard the word **cancer.** That's why I put this book together to prepare you a little and to let you know you're not alone. That's the reason Lolly Pop was born.

Andrea, aka Lolly x

How to Use the Book

We are all unique. Everyone will have an individual treatment plan and each of you will have different information to process. You might devour every statistic, searching chapter and verse about your treatment. Or, like me, you might bury your head in the sand, rising only to find out the bare essentials. Whatever camp you're in, you should find something that resonates with you.

Given the panic you are experiencing, you might not have the stomach to trawl through a whole book about breast cancer. You may just want specific information. That's why I've set the book loosely into three sections as people have treatments, such as reconstruction, at different times. It might not be in the chronological order you would expect.

Diagnosis - When you start your cancer journey: the uncertainty, the fear and the unknown.

Treatment - Once you are in the system: the options, the decisions, the impact and the changes.

Cutting the apron strings –The scary part when, once you have had all your treatment, you are sent out into the wide world with the words, *"See you in a year,"* ringing in your ears.

It's organised like this, so you can dip into sections where you need knowledge and information, leaving the rest until the next bump in the road is upon you. You will discover the treatment section is the largest, but don't be intimidated by that. This is where you will have most questions which is why it's the most extensive section.

You can, of course, read it from cover to cover. Whatever route you take, this book will hold your hand and help you navigate the various ups and downs of treatment.

Helpful Links and Glossary - I have included a *'Helpful Links'* section at the back which you might want to dive into, and for fun, there is a *'Glossary'* at the back that shows some fun definitions of words that will become part of your language. I've popped an asterisk by these.

'Stay on the bus'—what does it mean, and how does it help?

The shock and fear induced by the diagnosis massacred my concentration. I found it impossible to read the dry, cold and factual medical literature they gave me in the hospital, and it often ended up scaring me more.

The NHS and Macmillan staff were brilliant, and their pamphlets were packed with information, but I found them too much, as I was in no state to take much in. I have a whole cupboard full of unopened medical letters covered in dust. Every time I attended an appointment, I would see the consultant's mouth move, but the words would go over my head.

My best friend, known as Aunty Pyjamas to my kids, who is also a Macmillan nurse, gave me the best advice to help me cope with my diagnosis and treatment, which is, if you haven't guessed it, *"Stay on the bus."* She told me I was in the system and that the 'bus' would take me where I needed to go. It would be a bumpy ride, but to cling on tight as I would get to where I needed to be.

What she was saying was to have trust in the system. You might think it's only happening to you, but the NHS has dealt with millions of people just like us. The treatment you receive in the UK is gold standard, and they know what they are doing. I'm not saying there isn't room for improvement in an underfunded system, but it has your best interests at heart.

'Stay on the bus' became my mantra and helped me steer through the operations, chemotherapy, radiotherapy and anxious appointments while waiting on results. We will all have our own 'bus', and even though we won't be driving, it will get us to where we need to be.

I hate motivational quotes and here is one that I feel is nonsense—but I like it!

'Being drunk on a bus is not the same as being sober on a bus.'

~ Ozzy Osbourne

Contents

SECTION 1:

Diagnosis

A Little About Me and How Lolly Pop Was Born

The prospect of treatment terrified me, and I struggled and bawled my way through it. I was lonely and yearned to know more, but I feared the cold medical detail in hospital pamphlets.

So this is the guide I couldn't find!

I hope this helps you. I've tried to keep it light-hearted with just enough detail from someone who's been through it. Once I decided *Stay on the Bus* would be its title, it occurred to me that a lollipop lady could be my avatar. She could direct people with her giant stop-and-go sign, keeping them on track. It wasn't much of a leap to call her Lolly. I know you think I am on another planet, but it all made sense in my head at the time.

I'm not sure it translates to an American audience where they have crossing guards, not lollipop ladies (or men), but they don't have zebra crossings either.

My mind raced with how to promote Lolly on social media, knowing I would need a larger-than-life persona. I would also need a lollipop uniform, so I began to surf *eBay for second-hand outfits. Most were over £100, and that was for the sign alone!

I decided to look at fancy dress instead. Surprisingly, I realised there wasn't much demand for a lollipop outfit as I waded through the sexy nurse costumes. The closest I came to finding one was a Halloween zombie lollipop lady complete with a stop sign that said 'DIE!' and a tyre mark where she had been run over. I wisely decided this was entirely inappropriate for my audience.

There was only one option left—I would have to make my own. I stole my daughter's yellow ***Primark** sweatshirt, which was five sizes too small and had to be turned inside out to hide the slogan. It hardly covered my stomach, but as I planned to wear a fluorescent top over it, I could hide my midriff shame. A friend from the local council gifted me the luminous jacket.

To complete my outfit, I would need a fun head of some sort. Again, my mind went into overdrive, and I created a helmet which looked like an edible lollipop. As I said, it made sense to me at the time. I covered a beach ball in papier-mâché and then painted it pink. This was a nod to breast cancer—it was also the only paint my daughter had in her art box! It ended up being far too big, so I stuck the cardboard from a four-pack of ***Stella Artois** lager inside, which hugged my head and stopped the wobble.

My stop-and-go sign was crafted from a pizza box, while various felt tip pens were stuck to my daughter's drumstick with duct tape for its handle. Much to the hilarity of my family, I proudly modelled my completed outfit. My mother said I looked like an air traffic controller, but, at this stage, I was beyond caring.

Anyway, anyone who thinks dressing up in a homemade lollipop outfit to talk about cancer is completely left field, can I direct you to a fancy-dress outfit where you can dress up as a lobster?

Whatever floats your boat, I say. I'm thinking of ordering this for my next project.

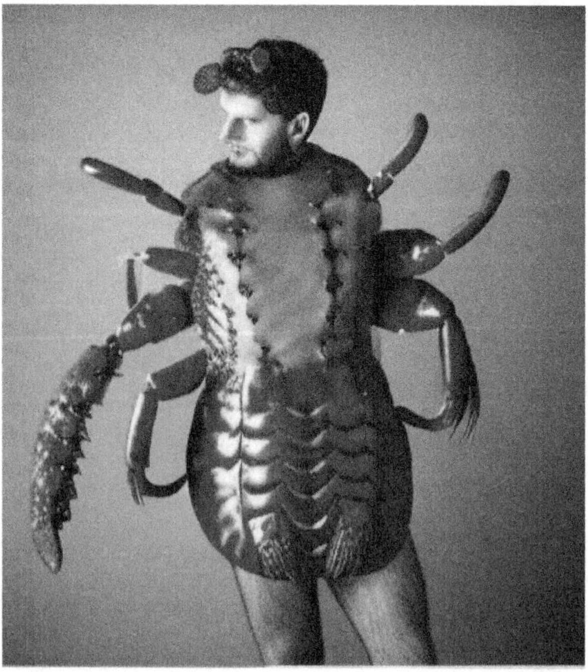

Finding Out

My Experience

Grade 3 HER2-positive tumour.

Even to this day, I find it hard to say the words. It was April 2019, and I found a lump. It didn't hurt; it wasn't red; it was just unmistakably there.

Finding out you have cancer is like being punched in the face. We all have different experiences of how we found ourselves in the system.

This is my story.

It was April 2019. I had found a lump, and to be honest, I wasn't that alarmed. My sister had a history of cysts, and I assumed, as we shared the same DNA, it was my turn to have them. I went to see my GP, who confirmed my self-diagnosis and told me it was a cyst but sent me off to have a mammogram just to be on the safe side.

I was working full-time with two kids and a house to clean, so I tried to put it to the back of my mind. I insisted on going alone because *it was just a cyst*. I skipped off to the hospital, pleased I was skiving off work and planning where to stop on the way home for a latte and a pastry.

As you have picked this book to read, you will have had the mammogram boob-crushing experience, so I won't elaborate. I was taken into a room and told the imaging machine wasn't working, so I might have to be called back. I didn't give it a second thought and gaily went off for my doughnut.

The next day, I received a phone call and began to have flutters of concern. This time I took my partner.

Bloody hell, I'm glad I did!

Taken into a room with two nurses, I began to panic. I'm sure you have already had your biopsy, so you know it's not pleasant. Even though the AK-45 biopsy gun shocked me, the unknown terrified me more. By the time I put my clothes back on, I was bawling and escorted to the 'quiet room'.

I knew I was in trouble.

I was joined by my partner, and we sat on the ***faux leather** seat waiting to see the consultant. It felt like an age, and we both looked at each other, expecting the worst. Eventually, the consultant summoned us. I felt numb.

"We don't know if it's cancer, but there are suspicious cells."

The worst thing is they can't tell you for certain. The biopsy has to be sent off, and the results take ten days—welcome to ***limbo land**. They tell you they have to confirm it with the biopsy results, and even though they don't use the word cancer, the fact that the Macmillan nurse accompanies the ***head honcho**, you have a fair idea that they know the answer already.

My partner and I numbly walked away and went on a crazy shopping spree, returning home with shoes, an aubergine, and a mug. Strangely ravenous, we then stuffed ourselves with an all-you-can-eat Chinese meal. I desperately tried to get hold of my best friend, but she was having her hair cut and not answering her phone. Exhausted, my partner and I crashed out and went to bed for hours in the middle of the day.

From talking to others, this behaviour is quite normal. My friend Clare went to Tesco and bought tins of dog food but doesn't even have a dog! Estelle, like me, ate her body weight in fry-ups. The shock not only messes with your brain, but your body needs added calories to process the shock. If you add a bottle of wine into the mix, I don't think anyone would blame you.

The Agonising Wait For Results

You will be familiar with the fear as it seeps into the pit of your stomach and your bones. You can't sleep at night or function the next day, and you wish your life away but, at the same time, don't want the day of reckoning to arrive.

People deal with it in different ways. No medication will help with this one, except, perhaps, something that knocks you out for a week. To cope, I manically cleaned like I was freebasing cocaine, which is not my normal behaviour. I also went out for one more massive bender at The Moon and Bell pub.

Shock

Is it shock? Is it fear? I'd say it's a massive dose of both. However you want to label it, it's something you have probably never felt before.

We all have past experiences that have filled us with panic. Mine include dropping £90 (not my own money) in the student union bar, missing the last bus home, reversing my dad's car into a post, leaving a drunken text—the list goes on and on.

One of my worst experiences was being entrusted with a child who had a severe nut allergy. I removed all traces of the offending ingredient from my house, only for my friend Baz to give the kids a ***Toblerone** over the garden fence. Yes, it contains nuts. I'll never forget the sweat pouring down my back as I phoned their mother.

Luckily for me, unlike my chocolate monster children, their friend had turned it down. Sensible and educated about their allergy, the child was super vigilant about everything they ate. In panic mode, I still made all the kids wash their hands and rinse out their mouths. I couldn't be sure, and for a few terrible hours, my mind raced with possibilities.

That's what it feels like to hear those words 'suspicious cells'. Unless you have felt that level of anxiety, you can't understand the fear you feel in your bones and core.

To help you through this anxious time, some might suggest meditation or deep breathing exercises, but at this stage, you can only hyperventilate. This is the worst stage, but it does get better once you start your treatment plan and get on the 'bus'.

Results Day

At last, after a ten-day wait for the biopsy result, at 5 p.m. on a Thursday, I met my surgeon. As you will discover, consultants are, on the whole, fairly blunt, but to be fair, if you had their job, you would be too.

They came right out with it. "We will have to remove the breast." There were other words, but the shock prevented me from hearing them. All I heard was, "Booked in on Monday."

The nurse over-compensated for the brusque manner of the consultant and grinned like a Cheshire cat. I couldn't absorb any more information and left clutching a bunch of papers, including various appointment letters. This gave me Friday and Saturday to prepare, but I spent most of my time bawling. I got up at 5 a.m. the following day, again, not my usual behaviour, and watched a 1970s Italian documentary about a man climbing a mountain with his cello. Concentrating on the subtitles didn't give me time to think and blocked my racing mind.

Friday was pre-admission checks and weigh-in with the sensitive observation, "You're on the obese scale." It was another slap in the face, but at that stage I didn't care—more bawling and then home to tell our twelve-year-old twin girls what was happening. We tried to soften the news with a trip to *__McDonald's__, but that's another story. (See the section, *'Telling the kids about your diagnosis'*.)

My treatment plan involved a mastectomy, lymph node removal and radiotherapy, taking Herceptin (a treatment to target cancer cells and stop them from growing and dividing) and hormone blockers. I felt like I got both barrels, but as my best friend said, "You got the NHS gold standard treatment, so shut up and get on the bus."

There is No Escape

When you are diagnosed, you see cancer everywhere. From the ghastly adverts asking for charity donations, *"A sister is still a sister...a lover is still a lover,"* to the main storyline of a TV show like Neighbours. Although, at the time of writing this, Neighbours is about to be cancelled— it was one of the main programmes that got me through. You cannot escape. It's everywhere you look. You become sensitive and a little bit angry. Even on Graham Norton's TV show, where you expect a laugh, especially when he's interviewing the late, great [1] Robin Williams, who talked about his latest heart surgery and waking up with wires hanging out of his chest and being spaced out on the drug they gave him, Propofol, nicknamed 'milk of amnesia'. Michael Jackson was taking Propofol to help him sleep, he said, which is like asking for chemotherapy because you're tired of shaving your head. And there it was!

Was there no escape from the constant reminder? Was I offended? Part of me thought I should be. Was he belittling my experience? No, it just made me laugh. I also like Robin Williams, especially as he named his daughter after a video game- Zelda. Now that's cool.

The thing is, cancer is everywhere: on the TV, radio, magazines in shops, people dressed in pink tutus running races, and those who shake donation tins. It always was everywhere, but now, you notice it more. It's normal to feel like you can't escape, but once you're on the 'bus', you will feel better.

The Blame Game

When you are first diagnosed, you will go through the 'poor me' and 'why me?' phases, and then you begin to blame yourself.

We all know that alcohol, drugs and eating rubbish contribute to bad health, and I'm not saying they don't play their part. But blaming yourself and lamenting the fact you were excessive in your youth doesn't mean that's what is responsible.

I must admit I went through all those emotions. My early twenties through to my late thirties were littered with late nights and drinking seshes. Once I got my diagnosis, I would start every day with, '*If only I hadn't….*' But beating yourself up is not the answer and is counterproductive.

'You can't keep blaming yourself. Just blame yourself once and move on.'

~ Homer Simpson (created by Matt Groening)

What made me laugh was that breast cancer used to be called the Nun's Disease. Now nuns are not renowned for their hedonistic love of raves, although my partner's dad talked fondly of a nun who used to come into his pub in the 1970s for a drop (barrel) of whisky. I think we can safely assume that the majority live a simple and pure life, with a few exceptions. The reason nuns were considered susceptible was because they never reproduce or breastfeed. Some studies back this up, but the general findings are it is related to oestrogen. I had twins and breastfed them until they were six months old, and I still got breast cancer.

So the thing is, blaming yourself is just a form of self-flagellation. You are where you are, and you can only go forward. There are plenty of people on their deathbeds wishing they had been more adventurous. You need your energy for what's coming next. The past is gone. Drop that internal criticism.

In the words of a '70s classic tune:

'Don't blame it on the good times.
Blame it on the boogie'.

~ The Jackson 5

Not sure what that means, but it makes me laugh anyway.

Priorities

Telling the Kids About Your Diagnosis

The first thing that pops into your mind is how you will tell your kids. It's bad enough to take it onboard yourself, but what if you have children? If you're having chemo, it's unlikely that you can keep it a secret, even if you don't lose your hair. Mum's superpower of doing everything in the house will be depleted. I was told on a Thursday and had my mastectomy by the Monday, which gave me three days to get everything together and tell the children.

My daughter's picture

This was my daughter's reaction to me telling her. I think it succinctly sums up all the emotions you go through in a rather impressive mind map.

At the time, they were twelve years old. I procrastinated for as long as I could, taking them to football practice, and as any great mother, I stuffed them with burgers and caramel ice frappes at McDonald's, something they see as a massive treat. I thought that bribing them would make it easier and they would be more relaxed. The cold truth is it doesn't matter what you ply them with—except perhaps ***Valium**. There is no easy way to tell them.

My partner and I took a deep breath and told them straight. We said we didn't have all the answers or know everything, but we would try our best to answer any questions they had. I have identical twins, and you would expect them to react the same way, but they couldn't have been more different.

One burst into tears, climbed onto my partner's lap and wouldn't speak to me for four hours. My second child became all grown up and stoic and sent me a long text telling me how they would be there and support me. It wasn't until two in the morning that she came down hyperventilating and climbed into bed with me. I told her what the plan was (as far as I knew), and we would get through it as a family.

We were given a comic book depicting chemo as a superhero heroically blasting cancer cells. The kids devoured it within two minutes as it was too young for them. It wasn't long until they had scoured the internet for more information. It filled me with dread, but for them, information was what they craved. I don't know how they are related to me. I just wanted to be told what to do and get on with it.

Unfortunately, the kids were reading the book *A Monster Calls* by Patrick Ness at school. It tells the story of a boy whose mother dies of cancer. It is a good idea to tell their school so they can keep an eye on any changes in behaviour or work standards. Their trauma comes out in strange ways. I found out a year later that one of my twins, entirely out of character, had punched a kid who said, "Your mum's got cancer." But I will deny it if anyone asks.

The advice is, be honest. Yes, it's difficult at the beginning and is one of the hardest things you will have to do. They will ask lots of questions:

- Can I catch it?
- Are you going to die?

It's important that they feel they can keep talking to you. They have permission to be angry, embarrassed, and frightened, and it's all okay and normal to feel like that. Once the dust settles, they will be much calmer. Kids are resilient. They will soon be back to their usual selves, throwing their clothes on the bathroom floor and fighting. Or is that just mine? I have lots of pictures of my two draping their long hair over my bald head like a wig. They both enjoyed dressing up with my false boob and wig and running around the house shouting, "Look, I'm Mum."

What To Do If Your Kids Are Younger

There are plenty of resources, books and videos to help you, and I have included a page at the end of the book which contains links to various videos so you can look and see which are the most age-appropriate for your child.

Whatever you decide to do, remember that you are doing your best. You will not get everything right, but at least you will have tried.

Prioritise Your Mental Health

Cancer has its own cacophony of language. Suddenly you are surrounded by adjectives all relating to the 'battle'.

Although I continually repeated, "Stay on the bus," to myself whenever things got rough, I still found the whole experience lonely and scary. Feeling pathetic is compounded by well-meaning people who describe your treatment as some sort of war.

"You must fight it. You are a warrior. You need to win this battle."

'Cancer isn't an opponent in some war game you can stomp out by mindset and determination.'

~ Nancy Stordahl

Having treatment is exhausting enough without the pressure to be brave and feeling the need to daub your face with blue paint like Braveheart before your next chemo treatment. With the pressure to eat a rainbow diet, stop drinking alcohol and meditate, it's all a bit too much.

If you want to lock yourself in a dark room, listen to ***Radiohead**, and eat a packet of Tangfastics, then go for it. You don't suddenly turn into The Terminator when you get a diagnosis. It sounds like pseudo-technobabble, but you need time to process it all.

I think we all need to go through the melodramatic stage akin to falling to your knees, looking up to the heavens, and wailing, "Why me?" I hardly lived the life of a vegan monk, but even so, many of my peers had been more excessive than me and appeared no worse for wear. As I say in the previous section, playing the blame game doesn't work, so there is nothing wrong with a healthy dose of self-indulgence.

Believe me, once you are in the system and know your treatment plan, it's so much easier. People might call you brave, but you don't have a choice. Just get on the 'bus' and let it take you where you need to be.

Telling Other People About Your Cancer Diagnosis

You will go through the whole spectrum of annoyance, anger, and irritation. Did I mention anger?

Even though you want to punch people, remember you would have behaved the same way as them before diagnosis, so don't get too comfortable on your high horse.

It's best to be prepared and forewarned with information so you can manage your disdain.

People tend to fall into the following categories:

1. The General Expert

We all know someone like this. It doesn't matter what it is—they are the all-knowing guru. You can stomach it when they drone on about the best electricity deal or how you ought to have used the latest software but telling you how to cure cancer is a whole new kettle of fish. Believe me, they will talk knowingly about what you need to do, which generally revolves around food.

"Eat a rainbow diet." "Eat ***turmeric** with every meal."

They impart this information by telling you they watched a programme on it or saw a post on TikTok. All you can do is remind them that it's not a teenage spot you can cure by rubbing a mixture of matcha tea and cabbage water, then finish by burying your head in the garden with a raw steak. Cancer needs strong drugs for a reason. I'm not saying that pharmaceutical companies don't benefit from us all being ill, and I know that they have suppressed information on the benefits of things like cannabis oil in the past, but right now, you need to listen to your doctor and take your medication. If you want to try cannabis oil or any other alternative treatment, talk to your doctor first to ensure it's safe.

I am also a bit partial to meditation, crystals, and talking to trees, so I'm not knocking it, but they aren't going to cut it with cancer. If you want to go down an alternative route, that is up to you, but I object to the ill-informed know-it-all expert.

Of course, some advice will be helpful, like staying out of the sun and drinking water, but it still doesn't mean that sometimes the advice gets on your nerves. Or is that just me?

2. The Medical Expert

"You have one of the good cancers."

There may be some truth in recovery rates, but it didn't feel good to me. I tried to work out why this annoyed me so much. Apart from being in a permanently bad mood, telling me it was a good cancer diminished my feelings and how I wanted to respond to it.

3. The Optimist

"You'll lose some weight."

No, you don't! The medication I was on made me gain weight. In addition to the chemo, the steroids, Tamoxifen, Herceptin, and generally lying around more than usual made me balloon. But I'd like to point out that having a flat stomach wasn't high on my list of things to worry about.

These people will also tell you how you have to fight it. I've already ranted about this, but you get the general idea.

4. All About Me

This person looks and gets all ***misty-eyed** and tells you how their milkman's sister's best mate's mum had breast cancer. They might go further and tell you how they died and how tragic it was.

You probably won't believe me, but this happened to me. It was the first time I had gone out to the pub with a couple of friends. I was bald but rocking my chemo hat and shades. While my friends went to the loo, I was outside trying to get a taxi. A very drunk tattooed man approached me and started crying, telling me about his mother and how she had died. Now I am not completely heartless, and I did sympathise, but I was, until this point, having a good time. I had forgotten about my diagnosis. He didn't leave for fifteen minutes, and by the time I eventually got in the cab, I was raging.

5. The Joker

"At least you'll get a free boob job and tummy tuck."

Now I include this category because some people found this very offensive. Having a mastectomy is major surgery, as is having breast reconstruction. People agonise about the type of surgery to have, and it's not something to take lightly. I have to say that while I wanted to be outraged, I actually wasn't. At the time of writing, because of the Covid-19 pandemic, I still haven't had my breast reconstruction, but when I do eventually get surgery, a flat stomach would be a welcome addition to my new boob.

How To Tell People

So how do you break the news? You can pick the phone up to a few people and let the jungle drums do their work, send an email, or announce it on Facebook. Whatever you choose, do it when you are ready. It's your news and yours to tell in your own time.

I had the good fortune to meet, if only virtually, Bettina Hubby, an artist based in LA. Before her surgery, she had the mother of all mastectomy parties and ended up having a whole art exhibition dedicated to her experience called *Thanks for the Mammories.* She also published a book of the same title, including photographs of the exhibited boob creations. Her website details can be found in the '*Helpful Links*' section.

Bettina didn't want the usual sympathy or shocked faces you get when you tell people about your cancer diagnosis. She sent a very eloquent plea on her Facebook page for people to send her jokes and things that would make her laugh.

She was inundated with a tsunami of posts, including jokes, pictures and art. The Facebook feed eventually formed the basis of her exhibition and subsequent book. The outpouring of creativity helped Bettina cope with the uncertainty and fear. Check out her story online; you will be blown away by how everyone rallied around creating amazing artwork of boobs from all sorts of everyday objects. She told me her mother thought it was very weird and almost didn't go, but she was glad she did in the end. When she eventually had her surgery, her mind was clear, and she faced it unafraid.

Compare that to me bawling in the ward!

You can blow up pink balloons, have a few friends around and bake some boob-shaped cupcakes, or you can go the full 'Bettina'—it's up to you. It doesn't matter, but it does help you reframe (to use a new trendy word) and help you turn a negative experience into a positive one.

Give Your Cancer A Name

Estelle Maher found it much easier to give her cancer a name and christened it Tracey, which was much more palatable for people than the word cancer. She found people could talk to her about it rather than skirting around the subject.

"Let's kick Tracey's arse."

Being the creative person she is, Estelle later turned Tracey into a book called *The Killing of Tracey Titmass,* where her cancer morphs into a human form and moves into her house as an unwanted lodger.

I didn't realise that naming cancer was a thing. My mum's next-door neighbour has a stoma colostomy bag and calls it Henry or her ***Tesco bag for life**. I wish I had thought of doing this and would recommend it as a coping method. I think mine would have been named after the bully at my school—you know who you are.

Practical Help

At this stage, you can start organising yourself because the next few months are fairly hectic. Presents are great, but people can help in lots of different ways. The thing is, people use vague terms like, "What do you need to do?" or "I'm here for you." The trouble with that is it puts the onus on the person with cancer. My wonderful mother duly arrived with a container truck of cleaning products, and my house has never been so sparkling. I had that help, but some people are embarrassed to ask.

People are also busy, so it's important to be specific when you ask for help.

- **Washing** – Especially if you have two teenagers like me who like to wear one item of clothing and then throw it in the laundry basket.
- **Cooking** – This was, without doubt, the most helpful thing for me. When my mother went home, my friend Monica brought chicken pies and spaghetti Bolognese to freeze. If you, like me, hate cooking at the best of times, when you are tired and slightly nauseous, it's a godsend.
- **Cleaning** – Keeping the house ticking along was all my partner could do. My friend came around and blitzed the kitchen for me, which was great as everything felt too much.
- **Transport** – If your hospital is miles away, as mine was, transport can be a nightmare. With breast cancer, you will have lots of appointments that will go on for about a year. Some you will be able to drive to yourself, but if lifts are shared among your friends, it takes the pressure off the family.

Also, as my friend who is going through cancer now commented, sometimes you need someone to ring you up and talk about something mundane like TV or give you the latest gossip. Sometimes you have to tell people to just be normal. You are the same person, but it's exhausting to constantly be asked how you are. Loneliness is very real when you go through treatment, and people can't be there all the time. Encourage your friends to text you. You don't have to answer, but it makes you feel like you are not alone.

SECTION 2:

Treatment and Side Effects

Mastectomy

As you will have gathered, the saying, "We will have to remove the breast," is also known as a mastectomy.

What is a mastectomy?

A mastectomy is a surgery to remove your boob. If you are brave enough to surf the internet, you will see different types of mastectomies depending on the type and severity of your cancer.

As I had a whopping lump, I needed a mastectomy and lymph node removal. I am not a doctor, so you will need to ask your health professional why they have chosen the treatment they have for you. They will look at factors like:

- type of cancer you have
- how aggressive it is
- your age
- if you are menopausal

I only had one boob removed, but some women will have both, which is called a double mastectomy. Others will have a lumpectomy which I will cover in more detail later.

Why do they do it?

In my head, it meant they were cutting cancer away, a bit like dry rot, which made me feel strangely more confident. As it turned out, it was absolutely the right option for me as I had five small tumours (I hate the word tumour), which they found when they examined my poor boob at the lab.

Lymph Node Removal

With the type of mastectomy I had, they also removed lymph nodes. While this was explained to me at great length, very little went in. In a nutshell, examining the lymph nodes can determine if the cancer has spread and how far.

Think of each lymph node as a tube station because the lymph nodes are in order, a bit like the Underground map. The cancer will follow a very distinct pattern, and by looking at the lymph nodes, they can work out how far it has spread. So imagine your cancer is travelling from Earl's Court to Turnpike Lane. It might not stop at every station, but it might have got as far as

Knightsbridge or, if you're unlucky, further along the tube line to King's Cross. The journey it takes doesn't change, so it lets them know if and how far it has spread.

In a rather technical process called preoperative mapping, they inject you with a slightly radioactive substance. That word totally horrified me as well. It allows them to take X-rays of the lymph nodes, so just keep repeating to yourself that it's there to keep you safe. Remind yourself this isn't the time to become obsessed with living clean. You weren't so worried when you were throwing snake bites down your throat at college.

During the operation, they inject you with a blue dye to help them map the lymph nodes. A side effect of this is that afterwards, your pee will be a bright blue. I half toyed with the idea of taking a picture and sending it to people, but that would have involved taking my camera into the loo, and I also thought I might get arrested.

Lumpectomy

This surgery removes the tumour and some healthy tissue around it. Unlike a mastectomy, where they whip off the whole boob, this pretty much leaves your boob intact. They remove a margin of tissue around the tumour to ensure that they have captured all of the cancer. Your boob may be smaller, but it will look similar to how it was before.

Ellie had a positive experience of surgery which resulted in minimal scarring.

> *'They removed the tumour and then moved some of my fat cells around to reshape my boob so that I didn't have a dent. They cut around my areola to get to the lump. My surgeon was very good, and he reassured me. I have a small scar in my armpit where they took out the sentinel node to check there wasn't more cancer. So actually, in terms of scarring, it is minimal. He's done a really neat job and I'm probably only half a cup smaller. I feel lucky compared to many others who have had much more invasive surgery. Being slightly smaller is not the end of the world.'*

Talk to your surgeon as we all go into survival mode. Ask questions about how your boob will look different and what to expect.

Recovery time

While having a lumpectomy is still surgery, you should not take as long to recover as you do with a mastectomy. You will probably not need a drain. Having said that, it's still a massive shock to the system and may only be the start of more treatment. Ellie had already had chemo and went on to have radiotherapy. We are all different.

Questions to ask:

- What will my boob look like?
- How do I deal with the dressing?
- When can I shower?
- Can I exercise my arm, or do I need to do specific exercises?

They will also give you a list of things to look out for. The most important of these will be signs of infection or seroma.

For some women, it's important to mentally prepare for the resulting boob, so make sure you have plenty of questions.

As always, take a notepad, or if you are allowed to be accompanied, someone can take notes for you. As I mentioned above, the lymph nodes removed will be sent away to be investigated, but you will have finished an essential bump in the road.

My Experience

Even before the Covid-19 pandemic, with all operations, you have to wash with antibacterial soap. It doesn't lather very well, but it is a small price to pay to keep infections at bay.

It is unlikely you will get any sleep the night before your operation. Lying awake hour after hour and watching the clock is quite normal before the big event. Not eating or, shock horror, not being able to have a cup of tea is much more difficult to take. Maybe it was the stress of waiting, but I would have killed for a hot brew.

The day of my mastectomy arrived. It was a Monday, and Aunty Pyjamas (not her real name), my partner, and my mum all came to the hospital with me. By 8.30 a.m., they were all kicked out, and I was left on my own in a waiting room with the other patients. Everyone smiles nervously at one another and watches the clock.

I was eventually called and led to the corner of the ward, away from everyone else. Gripped by fear, I howled like a banshee. Luckily for the rest of the women in there, the results of my MRSA test hadn't come back, so I was tucked away in the corner of the ward, out of sight but not necessarily sound.

A surgeon arrived, felt tip in hand, to draw an arrow pointing at my left breast, reassuring but scary at the same time.

The anaesthetist arrived, but I was too busy bawling to take anything in. I was so stressed that I forgot to puff on my inhaler before my operation, even though the anaesthetist had instructed me to do so. Even though I wasn't scheduled until the afternoon, I was wailing so loudly and scaring the rest of the ward, they wheeled me down early.

Waking Up and Pain

When you wake up, the nurses ask you to measure your pain from one (least pain) to five (most pain). I suggest you take all the morphine you can because eventually, they only offer you paracetamol. As I said to my nurse, "They've cut off my boob. I haven't got a bloody headache!"

Losing Your Boob and the Psychological Effects

Now I have never been a self-obsessed-Kim-Kardashian type, but losing my boob did affect me—big hair and big boobs, that was me, but not anymore. The nurse helped me shower, but I found it difficult to look at the wound.

Let me tell you, that feeling goes. Soon enough, you'll be making jokes about it. As my daughter said, "Are you an amputee now, Mum?" Prepare to be shocked but know the feeling will pass.

Be prepared to see boob shapes everywhere, from the pie in the hospital to rum baba pudding—you'll see them everywhere. This never goes away, and you will start questioning whether you have turned into some sort of boob pervert. I know, I'm a weirdo!

Hospital Food

Another thing you need to prepare yourself for is hospital food. The NHS saves your life, and they also have to feed you. They are much better at the former. The trouble is, good nutrition is vital for recovery. My experience varied considerably. The worst meal I had was a cooked breakfast, and I use that description very loosely. The bacon and sausage were swimming in a lake of tepid water, which sploshed onto my plate and bed sheet. The person serving it took one look and plonked a bowl of cornflakes next to me, conspiratorially whispering to avoid the cooked breakfast at all costs. I took her advice and advised every new admission.

Now I don't want to bash the NHS, but the quality of food helps recovery and helps alleviate what, for many, can be a traumatic experience.

[2] *'When a patient stays in hospital, they are strongly conscious of the importance of the food they are served – most patients told us it has a direct bearing on their experience and that the presentation of it affects how much they will eat.'*

A report, *New Blueprint for Hospital Food*, published in 2020, and launched by food and health professionals, highlighted the need for change. It's not just patients, but nurses and doctors who hardly have time to wolf down a sandwich and are knackered after a gruelling shift are hardly going to batch-cook vegan pack lunches for the week. Changes are needed, but so is funding, and they have had the slight issue of a Covid-19 pandemic to cope with as well.

Reassuringly, by the time I had my second surgery, the hospital had dumped the caterers, and the food had improved considerably. While the options for vegetarians or people with dietary considerations were poor, they did attempt to meet the cultural needs of the diverse hospital population. There were four different curries, which were very good, as was the cottage pie. The only trouble is once you have had it four times, it gets a bit dull. I'm not complaining. The NHS do their best with a limited purse. The catering staff, as always, are lovely and will ply you with biscuits and tea.

If you want a laugh, check out Bored Panda, where people post their atrocious hospital meals. The chances are, wherever you are, they will hopefully not be as bad. (See *'Helpful Links'* section.)

To be honest, food probably won't make it on your list of major worries when you have cancer. I have just included it, so it doesn't send you over the edge. A combination of steroids and fasting before an operation, coupled with stress, always makes me ravenous.

Going Home

It's amazing how quickly they kick you out of the hospital. In the 'olden days' (not quite sure when that was), the nurse told me that people would be in hospital for ten days. Now, some people are discharged on the same day as the operation!

After two days, I was at home, complete with a drain. This is a bottle attached to your body to stop the build-up of fluid near the site of your operation. Some patients have more than one. My mother christened it my 'Blood Bottle' as the liquid is red, and it was always referred to in a Transylvanian accent.

You have to measure it daily and call the hospital with the results when it measures less than 50 ml in 24 hours. When this happens, they will remove it. If you do need one, don't worry, it doesn't hurt. If you're lucky, they will give you a funky bag sewed by volunteers to clip over your shoulder.

Take your tablets and do what the nurses tell you, as you will soon be ready for the next hill on the 'bus', which might be chemotherapy.

Cording

Following lymph node removal, you may experience cording or, to give it its posh name, Axillary Web Syndrome (AWS).

What is it?

As its name suggests, some of us develop cord-like structures under the skin on the inner arm. Following surgery, the tissue surrounding the lymph, blood vessels and nerves becomes inflamed and scarred. Not everyone can see the cords, but you can feel them. For me, it was like someone had rammed a steel bar into my armpit. Every time I raised my arm, it was tight and difficult to move. It developed soon after surgery, but some women get it much later.

Treatment

Although the tendency is to keep your arm tied to your side, exercise is the key. The NHS gives you a series of incredibly dull exercises to do twice a day. The most exciting of these is the 'mountain', which finds you slowly crawling your fingers up the wall. Like all exercises, you won't feel like doing them and will find them annoying. I ended up making a recording of myself talking through the routine. We all hate the sound of our voices, but once you get over yourself, it will help. I found that without the phone playing my video instructions, I would rush everything and cut corners—sounds like my school report.

As you have been through so much, you expect to be in pain, but it doesn't have to be like that. Some patients recommend slowly massaging the arm and armpit. I never did this and would say always talk to your Macmillan nurse.

I felt like nobody took any notice of my cording. I'm not criticising my lovely nurse, Sue. I didn't really whine enough to her. I did, however, mention it to my GP, who didn't know what it was. As it's not life-threatening, I guess some parts of the NHS are more concerned with trying to save your life, so it's understandable.

But I have heard stories of women who were diagnosed immediately and sent to a physiotherapist to help with the condition. Your surgeon will closely monitor you after your procedure, so raise with them any concerns you have with stiffness across your chest, armpit or down your arm.

For me, it was one of the worst things about my recovery, and the persistent pain, even four years later, isn't totally back to normal. As you know, I like to be proved right, and I am not the only one to suggest it needs more attention.

> [3] *'Cording may seem a peripheral matter. Yet, from the patient's point of view, healing cannot fully begin while pain persists and arm movement is limited. Better awareness of cording among doctors and breast cancer patients will aid recovery and prevent chronic pain.'*

My advice is don't suffer in silence. Raise it and take action. It's yet another unfortunate bump in the road.

My Seroma

For those of you who were teenagers in the '80s, it's not that classic song by The Knack. For the younger, cooler generation, you can Google 'My Sharona' on YouTube.

A seroma is a build-up of fluid produced by your body after you have had:

- lumpectomy
- mastectomy
- removal of lymph nodes

It feels like you have a big, swollen balloon full of fluid under your skin—this is a seroma. They usually raise their bulbous head about a week after surgery or once the drain has been removed. They are not anything to worry about but can feel weird or, at worst, uncomfortable. The fluid is produced by the body, which sometimes can't reabsorb it. Your doctor or nurse will assess your seroma and decide whether to send you home and let nature take its course or if they should treat it. If they decide to intervene, they will make an appointment for you at the seroma clinic, where you may be met by an ***enthusiastic**

nurse who will rub her hands together and say things like, "That's a big juicy one."

Although it sounds horrendous, they syringe out the fluid. It looks like a pint of ***Newcastle Brown Ale**, complete with a frothy head, and it will shock you how much comes out. Having made you feel nauseous, I need to reassure you that it doesn't hurt.

As usual, keep an eye out for signs of infection. These can manifest as redness or feelings of warmth in that area. So, if your seroma feels like you could fry an egg on it, let your health team know.

I had to return to the seroma clinic four times before it calmed down. For me, it was just annoying, a minor irritation, so don't get too caught up on it.

Cellulitis

Although it sounds like a fancy sandwich spread, *'Cellulitis confit served with roasted walnuts and lightly toasted seeded rye loaf'*, it can be rather nasty.

Having had two bouts of it post-surgery, I am in a good position to reassure and warn you about it. Without freaking you out, it can be serious and does need to be flagged with the GP as soon as you notice it. It's a bacterial infection under the skin.

It manifests as a red rash that is hot or warm and feels tender when you touch it. I noticed mine when I was getting out of the bath, and I tried to ignore it but eventually went to the doctor.

The first doctor I saw thought it was a blood clot and sent me off to A & E, where I waited for five hours only to be met by a dismissive nurse who told me exactly what it was. A quick course of antibiotics, and I was fine. The second time, I confidently told the doctor my diagnosis, and I was right.

You are especially susceptible to it if you have had any lymph nodes removed. Well, I tick that box as I have had all mine removed. Lymph nodes are essential in removing unwanted 'debris' and toxins and things that can harm you.

> [4] *'The functions of the lymph system include transport of proteins (e.g., bacteria, viruses, cancer cells) and to remove excess fat, water, and cellular debris and foreign material'* – Andrzej Szuba

They describe the lymphatic system as a taxi taking undesirable things where they need to go. A great layman's description.

For someone like me who has had some removed, the remaining lymph nodes find it difficult to filter out all the bacteria and toxins, which could result in cellulitis.

It's vital to keep cuts and scratches clean. I can't even remember injuring myself, so be vigilant. Like everything, it is best to catch it early and seek treatment. Unfortunately, it can spread and become serious, so get yourself down to the surgery if you see any of the symptoms.

Have a look at the section on *'Lymphoedema'*, as many of the preventative measures hold true for cellulitis too.

False Boobs

Once the dust has settled and you have recovered from your mastectomy, if you didn't have reconstruction immediately, you will be offered a false boob or, to use the medical term, a prosthetic. Ok, you get a lightweight one when you have had your operation, but the new false boob is a BMW in comparison.

Like everything with the NHS, there is a waiting list. But when you get an appointment, they measure and advise you on size. They will then hand you a wobbly skin-coloured boob that comes in a very posh box, and you unwrap it like it's a wedding gift. They are realistic, feel like skin and have some wobble in them—like your very own executive toy or stress ball.

It's a massive shock when you feel how heavy they are. No wonder women with big boobs get back problems. It's like when I did the Alexander Technique (a self-development skill that teaches how to improve your posture and movement) when they told me my head weighs as much as a biscuit tin filled with sand. No wonder I have balance issues when I don't wear my falsie and walk into doors.

They also fit you for a bra. Gone are the days when you get your bras from Primark. Now you have to be correctly fitted. They ask you what you think you are, but to my surprise, I was about two sizes out. This is common, and it has been suggested, notably by Dr Pechter, that [5] *'8% of women wear the wrong size bras.'*

Apparently, in the intellectual study of bra fitting (yes, it's a thing), there is a suggestion that his work is flawed.

The fact that there are actual university professors who have dedicated their life work to how best to support women with their bras suggests we do have a problem. Check out Jenny Burbage, a bra heavyweight biomechanistic at the University of Portsmouth, who has made studying breasts (and how to support them) her sole focus.

> [6] *'There is no universal sizing system, and that's why a 32G Panache bra will almost certainly fit you differently than a 32G Elomi bra. Although they may be the same size on paper, they are designed for different body and breast shapes, so they won't fit exactly the same. These discrepancies can really suck when you're still trying to find the styles that work best for you.'* K T Babb

Not sure you would be familiar with a Panache or Elomi bra, but you get the general idea.

I don't think any of us are under the illusion that finding a comfortable bra is a nightmare. When we do find one, we wear it continually until it is battleship grey and frayed at the edges...or is that just me?

At least where I live, you are given one free bra and furnished with a brochure where you can choose additional bras. Prepare to take out a second mortgage because they are not cheap.

Mastectomy bras have pockets sewn in so you can pop in your prosthetic.

The first time it feels very strange. Your scar is probably still sore, and the weight of your false boob rubs against it. For me, the loose skin hanging around my back was more difficult. I found I could only wear the bra for short periods, and it did ride up.

The good news is that some hospitals have volunteers who sew in a pocket for you into your favourite bra, or you can do it yourself. This wasn't an option for me, as my home economics teacher at school could have told you. Some lingerie shops are excellent with knowledgeable staff who are used to measuring people who have had a mastectomy. If you can't find one near you, there are also many videos on YouTube with instructions if you are too embarrassed to speak to strangers.

While you might feel strange, take a moment to think about how people coped fifty years ago. They didn't have state-of-the-art boobs that mimicked the feel of real skin. I met an amazing older lady who showed me a beautiful blue silk pouch which contained bird seed. She told me she had only ever replaced the silk and found her homemade boob malleable and light. I liked it so much that I toyed with making my own.

Every woman you meet will have their own hilarious false boob story. My children let the dog get hold of it once, and we had to chase it down the garden. She was finally coaxed with a crust of a day-old pizza to drop it. To this day, my boob still has teeth marks on it.

Another time, I went to a wedding in Spain. It was hot, and I'd had too much champagne and wine. It was the first time I'd been out for months and had forgotten how to behave. Alcohol is not a friend to breast cancer, but sometimes you have to let your hair down.

After propping up the bar, I went to the ladies toilet. Meeting my sister and her best friend on the way, I began whining about how the false boob was chaffing. They dragged me into the bathroom and made me a false boob out of wet toilet paper. My sister used to work in the designer room in Harrods, and she created a work of art. The cool paper felt great against my skin and so much lighter. When someone knocked on the door, my sister grabbed the prosthetic boob, folded it over in her hand and we piled out laughing.

On the way back to the table, she was stopped by an incredibly stylish woman who said, "Wow! What an unusual clutch bag."

My straight-faced sister thanked her and shot back, "I bought it in Milan. It's a one-off."

"I can tell."

I have never been able to recreate that wet-toilet-paper boob, but perhaps the weather has to be hot, and you have to be drunk.

Following the impromptu bra creation in Spain, I began skirting the internet to find out how to make my own false boob. The internet is riddled with hilarious posts. I particularly liked one from blogger, DIY Marta. I've put her details in the *'Helpful Links'* section.

Here's the best part. All you need to make fake breasts are:

- Six tablespoons tapioca flour
- One cup water
- Saran wrap
- A latex glove
- Contact cement
- A small, deep bowl
- Hypafix medical tape

Given the cost of health in the USA, I am not surprised people are so ingenious. I spent a whole hour checking out her other posts. I particularly like the one on how to make reptilian makeup. I want her job.

I decided to give it a go. I would design it to be lighter in weight while, at the same time, satisfying my creative side. For a moment, my mind raced over how I could revolutionise bras for women before I quickly realised people have been trying to do this for years. Even if you have never had a mastectomy, you will have felt the pain of trying to find a bra that fits. We are all different shapes, which is why we need a proper fitting by an expert…duh.

Hours later, I found myself researching how to make a Star Trek Klingon breastplate out of papier-mâché. While it was a bit more ostentatious than I had expected, I was fascinated. I made a pact with myself to go to a sci-fi convention and make an awesome costume to strut about in. I haven't managed it yet but watch this space.

Given that my breast reconstruction surgery has been delayed for four years because of the Covid-19 pandemic, I rarely wear a bra. To be fair, we had lockdown, and I didn't go out. Having said that, I think I am at the age where I don't care—comfort trumps style. I still find that my bra pulls against my lymphoedema and makes me sore. I do, however, whack on my falsie when I have a business meeting or when I think men might look at my chest. Oh, that would be everywhere, then! But seriously, I am not as confident as I pretend to be.

There is a whole movement about going flat and embracing it. See my section on '*Tattoos*' where I also talk about the flat revolution.

Chemotherapy

Preparing Yourself For Chemotherapy

Before we dive right into chemotherapy. I warn you that this is a difficult part of your treatment and incrementally creeps up on you. One of the hardest things for me was to stop my usual rushing around and come to a stop. As women, we rarely slow down.

Let me give you an example of when I had a full-time job and spent my life driving from one place to another.

The night before an important meeting, I laid out my best trousers only to find one of the kids had spilt toothpaste down them. I don't know how they managed it as they were on the bed. Having Googled various cleaning hacks, I dried them on the radiator overnight and drove to work.

After an hour, I was still stroking my leg, congratulating myself on what a great job I had done. "Oh, that stain come out lovely." ****Woman's Own*** would have been proud. Only then did I realise, in haste, that I had put my trousers on inside out.

No wonder I could not see the white stain! Mortified, I changed in the service station toilets trying not to get them on the unsavoury urine-stained floor.

If you think that's bad, a woman I knew who had two cats would put her skirt on at the last minute so she wouldn't pick up cat hairs. She travelled all the way to Reading for an interview only to take off her coat and realise she was standing in her tights and knickers.

My point is life is super-duper busy. We rush, and it can be hard to do things at a healthy, leisurely pace. Cancer makes you come to a complete stop. If you were the sort of person who rushed around at 3,000 miles an hour, be prepared to find it hard. It's a lack of control.

Try and reframe your enforced rest periods.

Remind yourself of how jealous you are of ***ladies who lunch** when you race back from meetings to pick the kids up from school, throw tea together and get the kids to bed before you start your next job. You'd fantasise about the decadence of time, drinking a latte and reading the paper. Suddenly not being able to work doesn't sound so bad.

I began to look forward to it. Lying in bed, demanding my pillow to be plumped and my Weetabix cut into squares. While my butler trots off to find the grape scissors, I binge-watch *Netflix and sip Darjeeling tea.

The reality is somewhat different. The kids still see you as the fountain of knowledge, and to be fair, mine say I do have magic powers when it comes to where their school shoes, glasses and pencil case are when they're running out the door.

Teens quickly go back to their self-absorbed lack of empathy behaviour. My daughter told me she was now a 'young carer', but I reminded her that to be one, she had to actually do some jobs for me. 'Normal behaviour' is probably the healthiest state of affairs, despite not fitting into your fantasy.

Your other half is now responsible for everything. Some people are natural domestic gods, but in our household, Apophis, the Egyptian deity and lord of chaos, ruled supreme. He even has an asteroid named after him, and with the devastation caused by two teens, I can see why. It was at this stage the cavalry (my mother) arrived with an arm full of cleaning products and a slow cooker full of stew.

Parking

As well as all the drama of treatment, you will also have to contend with NHS parking. My hospital is in the centre of a city, and it is a nightmare to get to. Not only is the traffic adding stress, but having fought through the one-way system, followed by the inadequate signs, you often have to queue for the car park. Tempers get frayed when people try and push in, and the whole experience leaves you traumatised.

Entrepreneurial rip-off merchants have taken advantage of this by commandeering nearby wasteland and charging ridiculous rates. If you're late for an appointment, they are your only option. I spent my life feeling around the bottom of my dusty car seat for loose change as they don't take cards.

Despite my hospital trust building a high-rise car park, the problem of overcapacity remains. Before the Covid-19 pandemic, you would also have to find cash for the ticket machine, which was an additional STRESS. Now the system is all highly automated with number plate recognition. However, it frequently breaks down. Pretty stressful, and we haven't even spoken about parking charges. Expect to take out a second mortgage to pay, especially as breast cancer means you will have a myriad of appointments.

[7] *'The Press Association used the Freedom of Information Act to obtain data from more than 140 NHS trusts. The responses showed £254m had been raised during 2018-19 - up from £232m the year before, with hourly charges varying between £4 and £1 for an hour.'*

The same report polled nearly 8,000 people and found:

> [7] *'86% said parking added to the stress of their hospital visit. Respondents described the fees as a "rip-off", "extortionate" and "astronomical".'*

I don't think it needed a report to tell you that! Yes, I understand that the NHS is chronically underfunded and needs as much income as possible, but parking is a nightmare on top of everything else. At my hospital trust, I could buy a card for £50 worth of parking for £25. If you find yourself going to the hospital, sometimes daily for radiotherapy, check to see if there are any concessions.

As my friend, Aunty Pyjamas, said, "I'm staff and we have to pay too. Just suck it up and get on the bus."

If only there was a bus to the hospital from where I live, but don't get me started on local transport.

Preparing For Chemo – What to Expect

You might not have a Macmillan nurse. They might be called something else, like a cancer specialist nurse, oncology nurse or just Jill. Every hospital is different.

Don't worry. They are your go-to person, and chances are they'll be brilliant. If you are anything like me, as soon as you see a hospital uniform, you start bawling and nothing goes in. So when you get home and think of something you wish you had asked, you can call your 'Jill'.

Pre-chemo meeting

If you do have a pre-chemo meeting, take notes. Think of questions beforehand, no matter how stupid you think they are. You're more stupid if you don't ask the question. I was taken into a room and shown a rather tired presentation that they wheeled out to everyone. As usual, the nurse's mouth moved, but none of it went in.

The sausage machine chemo ward

If you expected a pristine, sanitised environment with gleaming steel, like an advanced medical spaceship, you might be disappointed. Masses of people of all ages sit around in faux leather chairs, eating sandwiches, samosas, bananas and drinking tea. My room was also extremely hot.

While they wait for your chemo drugs to be brought up from the pharmacy, you sit in a waiting room. Sometimes, they are so busy you can wait up to an hour. It's a good idea to take a book, Kindle or music with you. The only thing I took was a mascot, a Christmas angel decoration from the 1960s, which Aunty Pyjamas had rescued from her overzealous mother, who was throwing it out after a spring clean.

Eventually, they will call your name.

The first time I was plonked next to a man in a grubby vest, eating a yoghurt, burping and roaring, "Better out than in." This was the first time I realised the sheer volume of people in the 'cancer sausage machine'. I wasn't special, just another chipolata, although I see myself more as a cocktail sausage. But as my friend reminded me, you are in the best place, so shut up and 'stay on the bus'.

What happens during treatment?

Your diagnosis will determine what type of treatment you are given. The chemotherapy treatment I was given was FEC, a combination of three drugs. Now I don't know about you, but I was looking around for nurses to start sniggering. I felt like I was on an episode of Father Ted whenever the word FEC was mentioned. They also call it an 'infusion' like it's made in some fancy Parisian perfumery, but I found out later the nurses secretly call it bleach.

Having endured the usual drama of getting a ***cannula** attached (more about veins later), the nurse delivers a well-rehearsed joke of 'here's your cocktail' of steroids and anti-sickness tablets that you throw back like a shot of tequila. You find yourself lamely answering that you wish it was a real cocktail, and the nurse will laugh, humouring you as she has probably heard it a million times before.

Your chemo might be different, but I had a cannula with FEC pumped into me for about an hour. Bright red, you find yourself shocked by the colours. Red is associated with danger, and it has a visceral reaction making you realise how powerful those chemicals are. It looks like it would burn through a solid steel safe.

Try and have a pee before you start your treatment. You might have waited forty-five minutes for the drugs to come from the pharmacy. Once you're hooked up to the machine, it's a real kerfuffle, as my nurse told me, to wheel you to the toilet. Of course, this has the effect of making you instantly want to use the loo. Hospital toilets are never the most pleasant at the best of times, so try and avoid this inconvenience.

Hospital Toilets

If you're used to reading *Good Housekeeping,* you might have a warped idea of how hospital toilets will be.

> [8] *'Getting a sparkling loo is easier and quicker than you think. Here's how...Give yourself a head start by preparing the toilet before you begin. Squirt some bathroom cleaner around the rim and leave it to work its magic while you get on with the other jobs… Don't forget the top of the cistern; this can be a real dust trap.'*

In the real world, it doesn't matter how dynamic the cleaning staff are or how often they check the toilets, there is no way they can be there every minute. There is also the problem of other people.

I remember being desperate for the loo in the chemo ward while a man had used the ladies toilet. Not only had he left the seat up, but he had peed all over the floor. As women, we all know the issue of pee on seats and have ingenious ways of avoiding it by hovering over the pan and pushing the flush with our feet. Don't pretend you haven't done this because I know you have. I'm not blaming the man, well, only a little bit. Maybe he was desperate, maybe he had a disability, and despite the fact you think men can aim, I've been told, "It's not a precision instrument." Yeah, well, try being a woman.

The hospital I was in was old. The pipes were corroded blue and green, making them hard to clean. In my experience, the standard of cleanliness in the cancer wards was much higher than in others I was in. With the sheer volume of people in the chemo ward, the underfunding of the NHS, and the fact that people are attached to drips when they have to go, it's not surprising the toilets can get a bit manky. I'm not knocking the cleaners. Everyone I met was cheerful and worked hard.

You will have to share toilets. Sometimes they will be below par, but if you know that from the start, it isn't such a shock. My advice is to go armed with disinfectant hand wipes and you will feel a bit more in control. Because when you have to go, you have to go.

While we are talking about toilets in the chemo ward, it was only when I got home and had a pee that I realised just how shocking the FEC colour is. It's worse than the first time you ate beetroot and convinced yourself you were dying. But for a few days, your toilet will have its own ecosystem with acid rain.

Whatever chemo you are given, the advice is to use a separate toilet to the rest of the family as the chemical stays in your system for two to three days. But if, like me, that isn't always possible, then take what precautions you can.

Filgrastim Injections

So, having had your first infusion of chemo, you are given a yellow sharps box and a bunch of syringes. They tell you nonchalantly that you must inject yourself in the stomach daily.

Having experienced the drama of cannulas, the thought of injecting yourself seems like a job for someone qualified. Your stomach does not feel like a natural place to stick a needle into yourself. You are also convinced the layers of subcutaneous flab will not protect you from the pain.

When you've finished screaming, you will realise it is not that bad. Like most things, except for lemon curd, the thought is not as bad as the reality.

So, what is it?

The injection is called Filgrastim. The science bit explains it is used to help stimulate white blood cells, which take a kicking with chemotherapy. If your white cell count gets too low, you can become neutropenic (a weakened immune system), which can result in hospitalisation. (More about this in later sections.) It also helps to prevent or reduce the risk of infection.

How do you inject yourself without freaking out?

The nurse will show you but hang onto the written instructions to help you the first time you do it yourself. Remember, the first time is always the most stressful. As it can give you bone pain, the advice I got was to take it at night. I also set an alarm as forgetting or blocking it out of your mind is common. Take it out of the fridge thirty minutes before you administer it. Apparently, this makes it more comfortable, but if you forget, it doesn't stop it from working.

Wash your hands and disinfect where you will inject yourself, usually the stomach. The syringes already contain the correct dose, but it is not like a Calpol syringe. The one I was given had a small plastic piecer that you flip up, and then you can take the safety cap off the end.

Take a deep breath and clutch a bit of flab (the easy bit), then plunge the needle in. You will be surprised that it doesn't hurt.

Don't forget to put the used needle in your sharps box. Don't shut the lid completely because that will seal it, and, like me, you will have to get another one. While I waited, I put my used syringes in a jam jar.

You might experience some bruising. I bruise like a barrel of ripe apples. As women, we are quite used to unexplained bruises from a night out. They soon fade, and varying the side you inject yourself can minimise them. Don't worry if you struggle; this is normal and will get easier with time.

You can read the list of potential side effects on the label. I had bone pain, but if you read the side effects of paracetamol, you would never take it again.

Downsides—Unable to Ignore Withheld Numbers

A word of warning. Once you are on the 'bus', you will have endless appointments. The letters will pop through the post with regularity, and the phone will frequently ring with calls from phlebotomists, seroma clinic, chemotherapy ward, oncology, etc., and the list goes on and on.

The trouble is, the NHS withholds their number, so you have no option but to take the call as you can't afford to miss appointments. Gone are the days when you could dodge energy companies or companies with broadband offers, as it was usually them who withheld their number. Having treatment can be lonely, but the upside is that it's actually quite nice to speak to someone. As well as making sure you're not overpaying for your energy usage, it breaks the monotony. If you feel ill, you can always tell them to go away. Just take it as another unwanted side effect of chemo. It isn't going to harm you as long as you don't buy a new conservatory because you're bored.

Germ Paranoia

Who remembers when Covid-19 first started? Those from my household who ventured to the supermarket would have to remove their clothes and decontaminate themselves while I was out in the garden 'cleaning' the shopping. Tins and beer cans would swim in a bucket of diluted bleach, and I would meticulously wipe down the bags of vegetables. Disinfection wipes disappeared off the shelves as people bulk bought, so I used diluted Toilet Duck to wipe every purchase. The tins and non-perishables would be further quarantined for four days. I'm still finding tins I placed around the garden at the height of the pandemic.

Looking back, it all seems very laughable, especially as we had been told for years that excessive cleaning is ruining our immune systems, and there's nothing wrong with a bit of dirt. For people undergoing treatment, Covid-19 brought a whole new level of anxiety that I couldn't begin to comprehend.

Having chemo can lead to an unhealthy fear of germs. For me, knowing my immune system was compromised meant that I was terrified of people with colds. I have never been a Stepford wife when it came to house cleaning, but in your own domain, you have control. Other people are a law unto themselves.

I embarrassed myself, and my kids, by shouting at a man in Tesco. He cocked back his head and loudly, without putting his hand over his mouth, sneezed down my naked leg. I literally chased him down the aisle, telling him he was a disgusting individual. Mortified, my children melted into the cornflake display as I bought the nearby shoppers to a standstill.

As I told my partner later, it's not my normal behaviour. The man in question hopefully headed for the tissue aisle and learnt some manners. Looking back, I do feel a stab of embarrassment, but as I was wearing a chemo hat and massive glasses, no one would ever recognise me again. When you've got cancer, you can get away with anything.

Having chemo seriously affects your immune system. It's easy to see how becoming obsessed with germs could lead to intense anxiety. Of course, the scientists have a hilarious phobia label for it:

> [9] *'Mysophobia, also known as verminophobia, germophobia, germaphobia, bacillophobia and bacteriophobia, is a pathological fear of contamination and germs… Names pertaining directly to the abnormal fear of dirt and filth include molysmophobia or*

molysomophobia, rhypophobia, and rupophobia, whereas the terms bacillophobia and bacteriophobia specifically refer to the fear of bacteria and microbes in general.'

Of course, we must be vigilant against germs that could lead to infections. I will say be mindful if your behaviours begin to rule your life. Like all things connected to your mental health, talk to someone you trust. I think I could have developed all those things above if I hadn't recognised the slippery slope. Luckily, I had a best friend who was a nurse who sympathised and then told me to shut up and get on the 'bus'.

Preparation Before Chemo

I have already suggested how you can get your friends to chip in sharing lifts and cleaning. But there are things you need to think about. Before you have chemo, you might want to consider the following. A bit of planning can help when you get home and want to lie on the couch and watch Netflix. Things that you might not think of but proved invaluable to me.

I would not have coped without my travel mug. As a true Brit, a cup of tea always makes you feel better, except for my weirdo 56-year-old friend Caroline who hates tea and prefers cold drinks. Afternoon orange squash with biscuits doesn't quite have the same effect for me. Luckily for her, she also drinks wine, so we have managed to maintain our friendship. When you are in the midst of treatment, the effort of making cups of tea might feel too much. So get yourself a travel mug or flask, you can then drink tea until your heart's content. Mind you, the effort to make tea will be replaced by the need to dash to the loo. Unless you cut out the middleman and drink tea in your bathroom, it's an unfortunate side effect.

Drink water

Now I applaud people that can drink copious amounts of water. The younger generation seems to be permanently sipping on their mineral water, and good for them. The trouble is my age group is not in the habit of doing this. Perhaps it's got something to do with our feral childhoods playing out all day in all weathers, quenching our thirst with the occasional drink from the garden hose.

If you fit into this category, I am warning you now so you can be prepared. When undergoing chemo and most cancer treatments, you will be told to drink two litres of water a day—this feels almost impossible. If you fill up two litres to see how much it is, you will find it's the size of a small bath. So before you start, get it in your head that you need to do it. It won't be such a shock and will help you feel better sooner. Like all things that are good for you, it can be a nightmare.

My advice is to split it down into glasses to have throughout the day, like eating an elephant one bite at a time sort of thing. To be honest, it's probably easier to eat an elephant.

If you hate the taste, add fruit. Most people don't drink enough because they hate the taste. I have to say, I don't hate the taste. It just seems to be the volume. But as my brother said, "If it were a beer, you probably wouldn't moan so much." But even

I would struggle with a Stella Artois at nine in the morning. There is plenty of wisdom on the internet but also a load of rubbish, so be discerning.

Water bottles

Advice on the internet varies and is usually disguised as an attempt for you to buy the latest flash bottle. They range from ones where you plonk fruit into the bottle, where it infuses throughout the day, to smart water bottles attached to an app. The app reminds you when to drink and how much you have consumed. It does everything except drink the stuff for you. If you are the sort of person who loves technology apps, check them out. But I can't be bothered with yet another thing I have to upload.

Try and get into the habit of drinking one glass at bedtime and one first thing. Starting the day with a drink has a whole host of benefits if you are to believe the gurus on the internet.

After a good night's sleep, you may wake feeling dehydrated. Drinking water helps with weight loss and improves your complexion. The benefit of drinking a glass first was that it put a dent in the two-litre nightmare and got me on the front foot.

Stock up on ice lollies

When you feel nauseous and the thought of sipping, let alone drinking, seems too much, suck on an ice lolly. It was a tip a doctor gave me.

Food – plan your meals in advance

I know I have turned into my mother. My advice is to get someone to do it for you. I'm telling you to be prepared because once treatment starts, you will not have the energy to walk to the supermarket.

I am generally up for anything that encourages me to eat, but as we know, when you are having treatment, the thought of food can turn your stomach. Having said that, some foods are very high in water and sort of kill two birds with one stone. They also are high in nutrients and will get the thumbs up from your chemo nurse.

Lettuce: 96% water
Celery: 95% water
Zucchini: 95% water
Cabbage: 92% water
Watermelon: 91% water
Cantaloupe: 90% water
Honeydew melon: 90% water

[10] *'In addition to their high fluid content, these fruits and vegetables are packed with vitamins, minerals, and antioxidants that promote your overall health.'*

Yes, I had to Google cantaloupe too. It's a sweet melon and looks a lot more appetising than cabbage. I include these to try and help, but if you are like me and it's all a bit too much, opt for the ice lolly option.

Some people sail through chemo, and some have no problems guzzling down litres of water, but these little tips helped me. Anything you can do to make things less trying and reduces stress on your body is a winner.

Side Effects

Some you know about or can guess. You might get some of them, but you might not. Others you will know about, and some will take you by surprise. I don't want this to read like a terrifying shopping list. I'm telling you about them so you can be prepared, and they don't come as such a massive shock.

*Menopause

I'm mentioning this first because you will have thought of the other effects but perhaps not this one. It almost feels like an afterthought, especially as you are just getting your head around the fact you have cancer.

When describing chemo, they added rather flippantly, "Oh, and it will make you go through menopause."

I think they took one look at me and decided a woman my age probably wouldn't have any more children, so it wasn't a big deal. I'm not going to lie; it did feel like just another side effect, and I certainly wasn't planning on adding to my brood of preteen twins. Having treatment was bad enough without the monthly inconvenience, plus it saves you a fortune. However, I felt there was no discussion, and it was hardly even touched upon. It wasn't seen as something I needed to worry about; it was just another box to tick.

With your body being pumped with drugs, many women experience menopausal symptoms. It is called 'Men – o(n) – Pause' for a reason. Nobody is going to feel amorous being a big sweaty lump. Everyone knows about hot flushes, but until you experience them, nothing prepares you for the phantom kettle that blows hot steam at your back. You never quite know when the flush demon is about to strike. For me, while they happened throughout the day, they mainly happened at night. Waking up in a soaking wet bed is ghastly and cold, and it doesn't make for a great night's sleep for you or your partner.

Lolly Pop advice

Don't accept them as another thing; I admit I did, although I did moan relentlessly. If they become a real problem, talk to your team.

- **Alcohol**—Yes, just to suck the last joy out of life, limit your alcohol. To be honest, you probably won't feel like drinking anyway. Your nurse will give you more information, but it just makes sense to try and steer clear.

> [11] *'Alcohol can complicate chemotherapy by making mouth sores, nausea, and vomiting worse. It can also interfere with sleep, increase the risk of depression, and promote bone marrow suppression.'*

- **Smoking**—Again, not a great idea at any time, but if you smoke, try and cut down. Easier said than done, I know. I smoked eighteen years ago and only gave up after seeing a hypnotherapist. Before my appointment, I chained-smoked a whole packet in a field and thought I would throw up throughout my session. There are people out there that can help you. I'm not going to lecture you as knowing you need to stop and doing it are two separate things.
- **Silk pillowcases**—I didn't even know they existed, but my friend Eleanor swears by hers. They keep you cool and hydrated and even prevent wrinkles.

[12] *'If you've never experienced it for yourself, let us help you imagine a few experiences just as smooth, soothing, and relaxing as resting your head on a silk pillowcase:*

- *Coasting down a lazy river*
- *Gently swaying in a hammock*

- *Laying back in a field of fresh, green grass*
- *Resting in a perfect ray of sunshine*
- *Floating in outer space'*

Floating in outer space sold it for me. Now, where is my credit card?

- **Layer your clothes**—When the hot flush strikes, you can whip off your layers. In winter, I walked around the house in boxer shorts and a vest, shouting, "Look, I'm Lara Croft," only to be called Lardy Croft by the rest of the household. Who cares if everyone else is in down-insulated mountain jackets and snowshoes? If the central heating is turned off, everyone else will have to wrap up. With the ever-spiralling cost of fuel, it's a hidden benefit.
- **Plastic fans**—I know you probably don't want to use them in public, but they are a godsend, and you can pick them up cheaply on the internet.
- **Water**—Drink plenty and take every opportunity to splash your face. Not always possible, but water makes you feel instantly better.

- **Medication**—There are drugs that you can take, but talk to your doctor first, as they can interfere with other medicines prescribed to you.

Fertility

For some women, fertility is a real issue. If I had been one of those women, my treatment at the hands of the male oncologist would have horrified me. The best thing to do is discuss your fertility concerns with your chemo nurse.

I have put a section in the *'Helpful Links'* section at the back directing you to resources for information about fertility.

Constipation is Your Constant Companion

Embarrassingly enough, as this is for me to write, constipation is one of the most insidious side effects of treatment. You're not eating a large amount and are probably more concerned your hair is falling out, so a little dose of constipation doesn't sound that bad. Let's face it, you're having chemotherapy, for God's sake.

Let me stop you there. Out of all the side effects, I found this very difficult to deal with. Now I'm not talking about feeling a bit bloated after having eaten too much mashed potato. This is an all-consuming, arse-hole-bleeding nightmare. Out of all the things to deal with, it upset me the most.

The main thing is to prevent it, and if you do suffer, there are plenty of things you can do.

Diet

I know it sounds obvious, and eating isn't your number one priority, but what you eat does help. At the risk of patronising, the advice is to eat fibre-packed vegetables, such as peas and fruits. Prunes were a step too far for me, but if you are suffering, you will consider even eating these.

Liquids

The advice is to drink up to two litres of water a day, which seem like an impossible feat when you put them side by side. Splitting the water down into glasses and drinking them throughout the day helped. The 'eat an elephant one piece at a time' cliché does help. If you are already bloated and think another glass of water will make you explode, suck on an ice lolly. They feel like a luxurious treat after the sea of water.

Exercise

Again, whoever advised you to do 20-30 minutes a day has never had chemo. I used to drag myself to the shop at the end of the road and back again. Once you get out in the fresh air, you feel a sense of achievement. Let's face it, some days you will not feel like it, especially if you are bloated with constipation. But it's well worth it for many reasons, including your mental health and, most importantly, the benefit to your bowels.

Medication

There are plenty of remedies available for constipation. My nurse friend recommended Movicol, which tastes vile, but there are lots of medications to choose from. Your nurse will have heard it all before.

Keep a diary of your bowel movements. It's never going to be a best seller, but it makes you feel more in control. Also, if your medication changes, you might be able to head it off before it gets to the point where you're crying on the toilet—something I have done on several occasions.

If you struggle, talk to your nurse. She will give you help and advice. Be prepared to use words like 'stools' and 'bowel regime'. She will complete your humiliation by showing you a card with pictures of poo, and you have to point out the one that best describes yours. They don't have one that says like a 'giant rock' or 'granite'—both killers, but you get the general idea.

Nausea

Next to hair loss, the side effect most people associate with chemo is being sick.

Before starting your treatment, you throw back a cup of tablets. As well as steroids, they contain an anti-sickness medication designed to help stem the volcanic explosion. Here is a very boring list of all the possible drugs they can give you for the 1% who are interested.

- Aprepitant (Emend®)
- Dolasetron (Anzemet®)
- Granisetron (Kytril®)
- Ondansetron (Zofran®)
- Palonosetron (Aloxi®)
- Proclorperazine (Compazine®)
- Promethazine (Anergan®), (Phenergan®)
- Netupitant-Palonosetron (Akyzeo®)
- Rolapitant (Varubi®)
- Lorazepam (Ativan®)
- Metoclopramide (Reglan®)
- Dexamethasone (Decadron®)
- Famotidine (Pepcid®)
- Ranitidine (Zantac®)

You will not remember them but be assured there are plenty to choose from if one doesn't work for you.

I think years ago, nausea was an expected side effect, but medical professionals are very good at managing it now. Having said that, after my first chemo, I was sick in the kitchen sink in front of my eighty-year-old mother. She didn't seem particularly fazed and told me off for eating my dinner too quickly. I found this annoying and strangely comforting at the same time—she had a point. The steroids they give you can have you gorging at the dinner table, an unfortunate side effect they don't tell you about.

Everyone is different, and chemo effects can get worse with time. For me, this was true as my other memorable vomiting incident happened near the end of my treatment. Some people sail through while others suffer a lot more. Prepare for the worst and meet it head-on.

Tips for managing nausea

First, talk to your wonderful nurse. She's seen it all before and will give you sympathy and tell you what to do. The most important advice is to avoid things that might trigger you. For me, it was lemon curd and a huge advert across a double-decker bus for dog tapeworm medication. Stuck next to it in traffic, the juicy tape worm stretching thirty feet across turned my stomach on many different levels. Although my mantra is 'stay on the bus', that's one bus I would avoid at all costs.

Eat bland, dull foods such as crackers, toast, potatoes or rice. Ice cream is also easy to digest, which is probably why it's a favourite of heroin addicts. Have small meals, little and often. Try and keep some food in your stomach, such as toast, to stem the acidic volcano, and try not to lie down directly after eating for at least two hours.

While it's important to try and keep healthy at this point, the advice is to eat what you want. That sounds awesome, but if you're feeling sick, you won't want to load up on curry and rocky road cakes. It means eat whatever you like when you fancy it. Everyone is different; just get those calories in.

Smells can set you off too. So, obviously, someone else has to do the cooking while you watch Netflix. Of course, that also means cleaning materials trigger you, so get the other half to do all the domestic chores.

As always, drink lots of fluids even though it's the last thing you feel like doing.

If you've ever been pregnant, you'll know they advise ginger and peppermint. They sound like old wives' tales, but some do work.

If all this fails and you still struggle, your nurse can help by changing your medication.

Just to make you feel better, there is a YouTube video called *Justin Bieber & Top 5 Celebs Puking In Public,* which had 921 likes the last time I looked, so you are in good company.

Loss of Taste

It's funny, but having chemo makes everything taste the same, and you won't feel like experimenting in the kitchen with exotic herbs and flavours. My go-to food was tinned pineapple. Before I had breast cancer, I never considered buying pineapple. The fruit seemed impossible to cut unless you had a machete and arms like an ox. The tins felt like a 1970s throwback, something your gran would have with condensed milk or something you'd come across at the ***Brewers Fayre** on top of a gammon steak. Once I was having chemo, I found myself obsessing about it. It was a bit like being pregnant complete with heartburn, but my craving then was gherkins.

Why did I find pineapple such a good thing to eat when having chemo? I read somewhere that bromelain, an enzyme in pineapples, helps with treatment. For me, however, it was the taste. When you have chemo, your mouth is a heady mixture of metal and the bottom of a budgie cage. Pineapple had a way of cutting through that. Everything tasted bland except those cubes. Some people even put them in the freezer and ate them frozen. Typically, I only discovered that once I had finished treatment. My advice is if you're struggling to eat because of lack of taste, appetite, or nausea, give pineapple a go.

And no, I don't have shares in Del Monte!

Diarrhoea

Given how common constipation is, it seems bizarre that diarrhoea is also a common side effect.

You might not be able to spell it, and I'm sure we have all had a bit of a jelly belly from a dodgy kebab, but this is something a bit worse. I am not going to insult you by describing the symptoms, but it is important to keep an eye on it as it can dehydrate and weaken you. You might be familiar with 'through the eye of a needle', but if you're not, just take a moment to think about that.

Anger—How Do You Deal With It?

'Don't make me angry. You wouldn't like me when I'm angry.'

~ The Incredible Hulk

Obviously, I am practically perfect, like Mary Poppins crossed with a labrador, sprinkling love and happiness wherever I go. But having chemo resulted in me losing my temper and having a few out-of-character strops—a lot more than usual. This is completely normal.

I remember being pregnant and walking to the supermarket to satisfy my craving for gherkins. This was no mean feat, given that I was having twins and was the size of a small town. Having waddled home, I cried for two hours when I couldn't get the lid off the jar. Running it under the tap and throwing down my towel, I rang my partner in hysterics.

"But I just want a gherkin!"

Everyone found this hilarious, and it was put down to my raging hormones exacerbated by the fact I was having twins. It would all soon pass.

Chemo saw the return of the gherkin monster. I shouted at a man who had come to read the gas meter because he rang the doorbell when I was asleep. Furious with someone cycling on the pavement, I told them what a road is. Irritability became my normal state of being for a while, and my children and partner gave me a wide berth. I'm not proud of how I behaved, but talking to Sue, my lovely Macmillan nurse, I began to unravel why.

Anger is a natural response to the emotional impact of having a cancer diagnosis. Nobody is going to be singing from the rooftops. You have every right to ask, "Why me?" especially if you haven't led a life of debauchery and risky behaviour. In fact, I would say a bit of shouting and bawling gets it out of your system. But if you feel it's more than that, you need to seek help.

Medication

Uncharacteristic behaviour can also be a result of medication. While having chemo, most women are given steroids, and the 'cocktail' they give you before chemo does more than make you reach for the biscuit tin.

One side effect of steroids is that it can affect your mood making you irritable or angry. This is rather hilariously labelled 'roid rage.'

> [13] *'A general rule of thumb is that if your mood changes are impacting your quality of life or the health of your relationships, you should talk to your oncology team.'*

I quite like the idea of roid rage. I'd have liked a T-shirt with 'Watch out! I've got roid rage!' instead of a pink ribbon pictured across my chest.

The good thing is that medication can usually be changed. The advice is always to talk to a professional who will be able to manage any cessation or change safely.

However, anger can also be a symptom of depression. Please see the section '*Depression*'.

Thrush

This was a big one, and I never saw it coming.

'The day of fire is coming, the thrush will fly ablaze like a little sky rocket...'

~Anne Sexton

Believe me, there is nothing poetic about thrush. As teenagers, we were all appalled the first time we got thrush. It was nothing that a good dose of Canesten, or natural yoghurt, wouldn't sort out. Well, guess what? You have never had real thrush until you have had chemo. Thrush is one of the side effects that most are not warned about.

Mouth Thrush (Oral Thrush)

Horror, yes, you can get it in your mouth. It's a disgusting white mess on your tongue. The thought of it is much worse than the reality. Not great for making you irresistible, but let's face it, you're not going to feel like ***snogging** anyone anytime soon. However, it is extremely easy to get rid of with a few drops of Nystatin for a week. So don't worry.

There's more....

It likes to inhabit anywhere warm.

Thrush can become more insidious. In addition to the 'normal places', no one tells you that you can get the most appalling itchy arse. I'm telling you, so you don't have to have that hushed conversation with your pharmacist. No matter how horrified you are, there is an easy fix with Canesten cream (Clotrimazole). It usually takes about seven days to clear up and begins to soothe the pain fairly soon after first use. You'll be glad you bought it.

A great piece of advice I was given before chemo is to get separate towels for your top and lower half. Mentally this helps you cope better with the words 'fungal infection'. Remember, thrush is just your body telling you it's feeling a bit rundown—not surprising at all, but remember, it's easy to fix.

Mouth Ulcers

As well as mouth thrush, you can suffer from mouth ulcers. You won't be allowed to go to the dentist to have your teeth cleaned, so oral hygiene is paramount. Like most things, prevention is better than cure. First, buy a soft toothbrush. It might feel incredibly limp and useless, but you don't want to cause any scratches. Also, keep it separate from everybody else. You never know if someone has dropped theirs in the bin or toilet. (Have I told you about my children?)

Wash your mouth out morning and night with a medicated mouthwash. Regular mouthwash isn't going to cut it. It would help if you had Corsodyl or chlorhexidine oral rinse. I enjoyed the industrial taste as it's the closest thing you get to a quick snifter of alcohol. (To be honest, I don't think it contains alcohol.) The old lush that I am, I looked forward to my dram every night and morning.

I never had any mouth ulcers, but I met plenty of people who did. So, remember, a swig a day keeps the ulcers away. If you are unfortunate enough to get them, they recommend avoiding hot and spicy foods. As always, alcohol and smoking can aggravate them, so again, try and refrain. You won't be the first person to get them, so speak to your nurse. It's just another bump in the road. Don't suffer in silence.

How to Cope with Losing Your Hair

This is the area everyone freaks out about and causes the most trauma.

You don't wake up and suddenly find you're bald; it doesn't follow a predictable trajectory. It's not like you have the treatment, and then it miraculously comes back thick and voluptuous. Losing your hair and its regrowth is an evolutionary process. Instead of taking thousands of years, it transitions through several stages and takes about a year to get back to normal—and you may have a new normal. There are no guarantees with hair loss. Some people never regain it, but the majority will.

Let's start at the beginning.

You will find yourself trying to ignore the clumps of hair in your comb and the fact that the shower tray seems perpetually blocked. But eventually, you have to succumb to the fact your hair is going, and it's going fast.

I didn't lose my hair initially for two to three weeks. I was having a tantrum in the hospital car park, having lost my parking ticket, and was waiting for my partner to get another one when I started pulling clumps of hair out, and I let them go to float away with the wind. Deeply unpleasant for anybody in the nearby vicinity, but it seemed quite poetic and horrifying all at the same time. When we got home, we drove straight to a male barber and had all my hair shaved off with a number one blade.

The idea was to regain control of the process and own it. I knew motivational-pseudo-bullshit advice was rubbish, but I had to do something. It wasn't quite the empowering experience I was hoping for. I bawled my head off while lots of customers and random people gathered to stare and point.

Once it was done, it was done, and after a while, I did start to feel better. My newfound barnet also sparked a great conversation with a bunch of bald, middle-aged builders who gave me advice on wearing sun cream.

Hair loss is something that most people associate with cancer, and you can't ignore it. Unless you have a cold cap, you will be affected somehow. Not everyone loses it all, but I did, and like me, you will initially struggle with it.

Evolution of hair loss

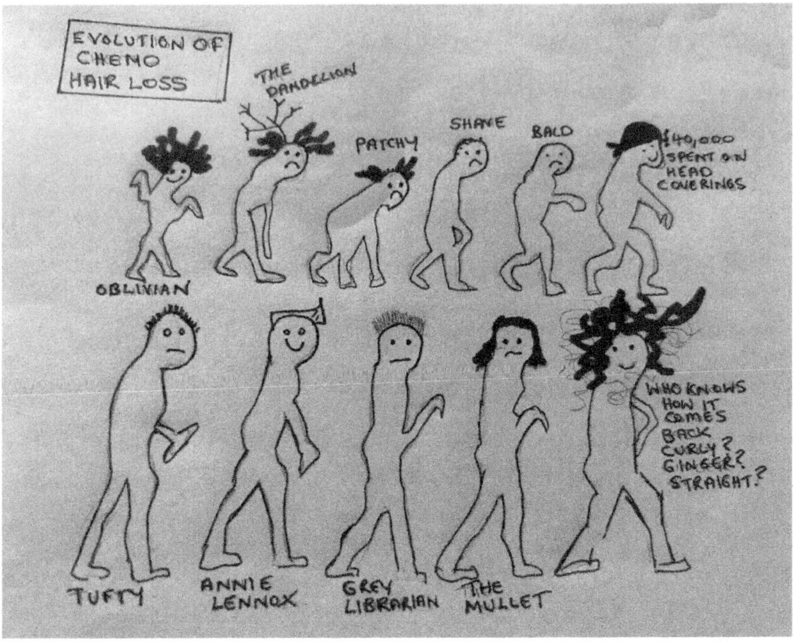

We are all familiar with the picture of the evolution of man from primate to modern homo sapien as a distinct species. This process took over six million years. I have applied the same principle to hair loss, although this is probably more like six months to a year. It may vary from person to person, but it follows the same basic pattern, or at least this is how it happened to me.

Oblivion—Pre-diagnosis and chemo, we moan about our hair being too curly / straight / dry. We gaily slap on chemical-heavy products and grumble about whether you need to get it cut again.

Dandelion—This is when you start treatment, and your hair begins to come out in wisps.

Patchy—The horrible realisation that you are definitely losing your hair. As you run your hand through, large clumps begin to fall away. Your head will take on the appearance of a logged Amazon forest.

Shaven—Given your appearance, it's time to take the plunge and head down to the local barbers for a number one.

Bald—This speaks for itself.

Tufty—Your hair begins to come back in tufts. I had a line at the back of my head like an old man's. The skin begins to be covered in a down of grey tufts.

Annie Lennox—This is a great phase. Your hair comes back white, and because it's growing short, it's the crew cut you were never brave enough to have.

Grey Librarian—The worst stage when your hair comes back grey and is still short. You have very little control; it's dull and has to be endured.

The Mullet—Yes, this is the 1980s hairstyle we all have to go through—waiting for the front to catch up with the back.

Hair! —Your hair might come back any way it feels like. Mine was once a mop of curls but came back straight. Some say their hair comes back ginger or wavy. It is exciting, and at last, you start to feel normal.

However depressed you get about the colour of your hair, remember your body has been battered, and your hair is fragile. No matter how much you hate the grey librarian, wait at least six months before you reach for the dye bottle.

Not everyone loses their hair, especially if you use a cold cap.

Cold caps

You might be offered or are considering a cold cap. For some people, they are great and work well. But there are no guarantees. I couldn't be bothered, and I got irritated with making yet another decision. I just wanted to be told what to do.

My friend endured a cold cap for several weeks but ultimately gave up. Others have succeeded with them. Talk to your nurse and make up your own mind.

Psychological effects

For some, the thought of losing their hair is a desperately stressful thing. I met a woman who had spent £3,000 on a real hair wig, and it cost £800 to regularly re-thread it. This would be out of most people's price range, but for her, it was important. If that's what you want to do, go for it. Don't beat yourself up for struggling with hair loss. It's more difficult for some than others.

Talk to your nurse about how you are feeling. You won't be the first to have a wobble, and they can help put your mind at rest. Remember, for most, it is only temporary. It feels shocking, but you do get used to it.

Wigs

You can get wigs from Macmillan and some hilarious online shops for £5. My kids were delighted to buy me bright pink and blue ones. Encourage them because seeing Mum being bald can be quite hard. (But remind them YOU are the centre of attention.)

Chemo hats vs wigs

While it may be true that some women can rock a bald head (think ***Sinead O'Connor** or Skunk Anansie), I have to say, if you're not under twenty, you might want to consider alternative headwear.

First, don't buy a chemo hat from dodgy eBay sites. My sister bought me a bundle of funky headwear that arrived three months after my hair had grown back. Also, they were so small they would have only fitted a ***Tiny Tears doll**.

Personally, I preferred a chemo hat to a super-itchy wig. I had a wig that Macmillan paid for; otherwise, they were about £90. Or, like the woman above, you can buy one made from real hair.

At an appointment with a 'wig lady', I took a friend with me, and we tried on lots of different styles, including a massive blonde Dolly Parton wig—a personal favourite of mine. Although I have always had big '80s curly hair, I wasn't sure I could pull it off.

To be honest, the choice was limited. They were all synthetic, and I settled on one that was straight and brown to make me look as natural as I could muster. I then went into The Range shop and bought a large and badass pair of glasses to carry off the look.

For your 'comfort', you also get a thing to wear under your wig. It looks like the gusset from a pair of beige tights, and I have to admit that I lost it almost as soon as I got it. To be honest, I hated my wig and only ever wore it to parents' evening. The rest of the time, I rocked my chemo hat and shades. My mother told me off for criticising my wig. She reminded me that my grandmother, born in 1906, had contracted ringworm and had been bald all her life. Her wigs were made of horsehair, and as there was no NHS, she had to spend a fortune. My wig would be casually tossed in the corner, where my grandmother would have treated hers respectfully. It never held her back as she rode her motorbike, never complaining. Duly chastised, I invested in a wig stand and promised to be more grateful and careful with my wig. However, my daughter wore it to school on World Book Day.

When it comes to cool head ties, some people have the knack, and some don't. I was clearly in the second category. My sister would grab a headscarf and, like magic, turn it into a super cool 1940s land girl vibe. I was all fingers and thumbs when I tried, and it soon fell apart and looked ridiculous. There are plenty of videos on YouTube which give you step-by-step instructions on different ways to style a head covering. I just stuck to my chemo hat. (See the *'Helpful Links'* section.)

Benefits of being bald

The benefits of being bald are that you are now a master of disguise. Once, I collected a DHL parcel from the local delivery point, which happened to be a dry cleaners. I hadn't realised you needed a passport and ended up having an embarrassing strop at the woman behind the counter. In my defence, she was horrible, what I would call a desperate baggage, but still. The next day, I returned with my wig on, and she never recognised me. Could be a good trick if you want to rob your local bank, but the only trouble is you probably won't feel like robbing one at the moment.

One of the most fantastic things about writing about your cancer journey, as well as everyone telling me how cathartic it will be, is the hilarious things you come across during research. I have already mentioned you lose head hair and eyebrows, but you lose hair everywhere—and I mean everywhere!

Being slightly uptight, I pondered how to write about this without offending myself or my mother. I did a bit of googling, and it took me down a fantastic rabbit hole about the history of pubic hair and women's relationship with it. Please indulge the historian in me and remember you will join a proud lineage of hairless women.

> [14] *'Because they considered a bush uncivilized, ancient Greek lady removed it by singeing and plucking. Upper-class Roman women took care of business using tweezers, pumice stones and depilatories, while women in ancient Persia used early hair-removal creams. In ancient Rome, how much hair you had down there became a symbol of status: the less you had, the fancier you were considered. Given how frequently they went to public baths, I'm guessing this was a major subject of gossip in the change rooms.'*

God, how I wish I had written this article. So women having chemo would be considered posh. Having read up on Roman baths and how unhealthy they were, I wouldn't suggest taking it any further. Reading with fascination that the big '70s bush is making a comeback, if you are of the persuasion where this doesn't float your boat, chemo will save you a fortune at the salon.

Other fascinating thing I came across was the Merkin which is a pubic wig. It dates back as far as the 1450s and were particularly popular among sex workers who shaved their pubic hair because of lice.

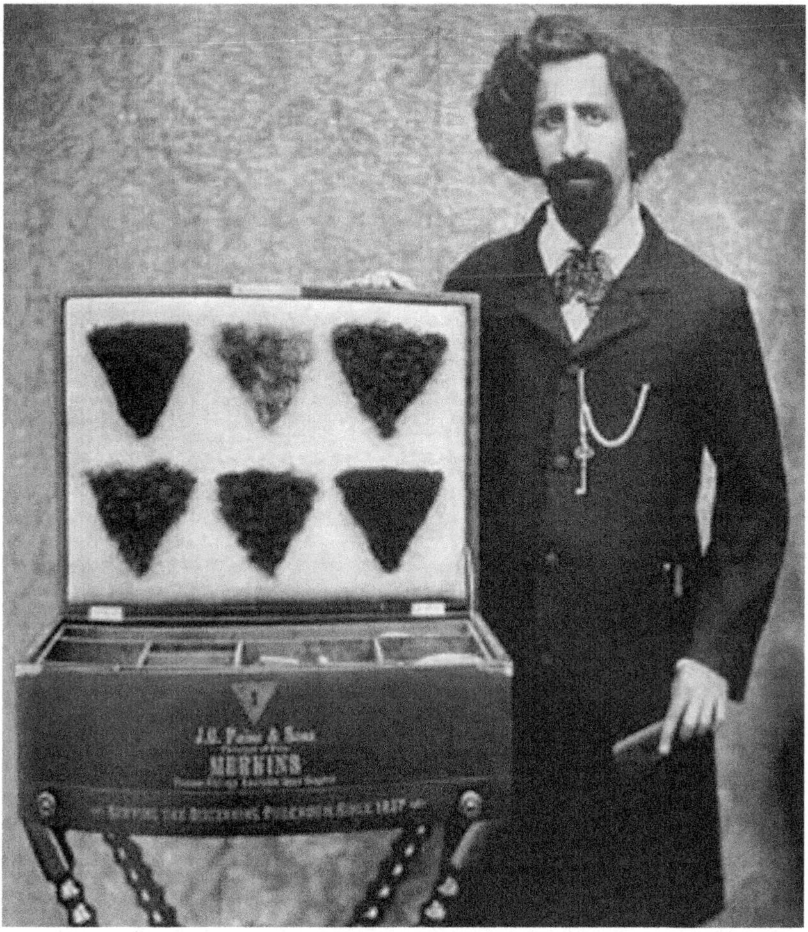

A salesman 'serving the discerning pudendum since 1827' yes it was actually a thing.

Eyebrows and makeup

When you do have chemo and lose your hair, it can affect your self-esteem, and you shy away from going out. You know that you will go bald, but you never really think about losing your eyebrows and eyelashes and what might happen to your skin.

I found ***parents' evening** particularly trying as I knew my children wanted me to look 'normal'. Whacking on my nylon wig wasn't going to cut it. This is when you stare at yourself in the mirror, clock your puffy, red eyes, dry, blotchy skin and lack of eyelashes and realise that gives you an air of alien demure. Given the enormity of your diagnosis, the complexities of what makeup to apply seems trivial and self-obsessed. I was lucky enough to get a place on a 'Look Good. Feel Better' workshop. They describe themselves as a leading cancer support charity aimed at boosting the physical and emotional well-being of people living with cancer. They provide workshops: covering skincare and make-up, grooming, hair loss, hair care, wig advice and nail care. I have put their details in the *'Helpful Links'* section.

Underfunded, as all charities are, there were limited places, and I had to wait three months before I found myself in a room with ten other women, all clutching gift bags of surprisingly posh goodies of makeup and perfume. The volunteers take you through practical steps of how to apply foundation, eye makeup and skincare products. As I had an eye infection, I sat out for some of it, but it was fun to watch everybody else. The most hilarious thing was drawing on eyebrows. You might think this is easy. Think again! The team of volunteers, who are all makeup professionals, spent ages meticulously showing us how to do it. It all looked easy and seamless—then it was our turn.

Shakely holding the pencil, we tried to follow the contour of our eyes as we had been instructed. Triumphantly, the woman next to me threw down her brow pencil and asked me what I thought of her attempt. Without thinking or trying to hide my horror, I blurted out that she looked really evil!

Heavy-handed and inept, we looked like a permanently surprised bunch of ***pantomime villains**. Luckily, she had a sense of humour, and we spent the next ten minutes in hysterics. To be honest, the experience of meeting other women and having a laugh was just as valuable as the makeup lessons.

If you want to contact the charity, their details are in the *'Helpful Links'* section at the end of this book. They also do online classes.

Now I have never been particularly interested in the latest makeup and would not consider myself an expert, but here are plenty of excellent videos on YouTube giving you step-by-step instructions on how to apply it and what products work best.

Check out the Cancer Hair Care website (contact details in *'Helpful Links'*), which has a whole section on how to apply false lashes—something I never even attempted to do. Like all things, this period will pass, and you just need to 'stay on the bus'.

Conjunctivitis or 'Pink Eye'

Another unfortunate side effect of chemo is conjunctivitis. When you wake up, your eyes feel gritty. You stumble to the bathroom mirror and are shocked that your eyelids are stuck together with something disgustingly crusty. Once you manage to prise them open, your pink eyeballs look like you've drunk a whole bottle of ***Jack Daniels** and turned into a hungover demon.

So what is it?

As horrible as it sounds, it's merely an inflammation and infection of the see-through membrane that lines your eyelid and eyeball. Difficult as it is, try not to rub your eyes and, if you have to, make sure your hands are clean.

Dampen a ball of cotton wool and dab it around the area. It should help to remove some of the discharge and help relieve the discomfort. I found that placing a cold compress of cotton wool over the eye also helped. Pretend it's cucumber, and you're at a posh health spa if it helps.

If it doesn't seem to be clearing up or you are worried, your doctor may prescribe some antibiotic drops depending on the severity. It's a good idea to avoid makeup and not wear contact lenses. Protect everyone else in the family by using separate towels and pillowcases. You will be doing this anyway but keep your hands clean and away from your face—easier said than done.

Watery Eyes

While we are on the subject of eyes, I also suffered from watery eyes. They would stream uncontrollably; although I'm known for my excessive bawling, this was different. It sounds like an oxymoron, but watery eyes can signify dry eyes. Yes, I know! This is when the tear ducts don't produce enough of a chemical which helps lubricate your eyes. Again, your eyes feel gritty and dry. Like pink eye, your doctor can give you drops that can help.

Vision

If you get harassed by your optician because your yearly check-up is due, you can legitimately tell them that chemo can affect your vision, so they will have to wait.

[15]'Many cancer treatments, including chemotherapy, radiation, steroids and immunotherapies, are known to cause eye-related side effects such as dryness, tearing, cataracts, sensitivity to light, infection or altered vision. It's even possible for eye colour to change.'

In most cases, this is only temporary but something to bear in mind. As always, the advice is to talk to your nurse and treatment team.

Nails During Chemo Treatment

Remember the words 'might', 'may', and 'sometimes'. Not everyone is affected to the same degree.

Another side effect of treatment is your nails. I had a total tantrum when I realised that I would not only lose my hair, eyebrows and spend my life constipated, but I could also get black nails.

Perhaps the worst aspect of chemo is that your nails look bruised, like you've dropped a saucepan on them. Imagine a bruise that changes like a rainbow to various stages of black, blue, purple and green.

No amount of eating jelly (something I was advised to do as a child to promote nail growth) is going to help. Your nails become brittle, and unless you sit on your hands all day, they will break easily. In fact, sitting on them probably isn't a good idea, either. You can also get horizontal and vertical lines. A bit like tree rings showing the different cycles of chemotherapy.

WARNING! Read this bit quickly. Sometimes the whole nail can lift away from the nail bed and fall off. I know you are saying yuck in your head, but it's important to know in case it becomes infected.

I advise taking it on the chin and remembering it's not forever. Whatever colour your nails go, they will grow out. Having said that, I wasn't that stoic. Of course, it's horrible and another smack in the face, but it will pass. Black nails have long been championed by ***Goths**. Remember listening to Siouxsie and The Banshees? She managed to rock a name like Susan. She would embrace black nails, and you should too. Now I'm not suggesting you change your whole wardrobe to black. Just keep reminding yourself it's a bump in the road, 'stay on the bus', and it will pass.

I know whatever I say, it still isn't something you wanted or expected, but there are things you can do to help.

Prevention is best

- Wear gloves all the time when washing up or gardening. Not such a big deal as you probably do it anyway. Try and keep your hands out of water as much as you can.

- Don't go and have a massive manicure where they cut the cuticles and use gel that needs an acetone remover. This will seriously mess up your nails.
- False nails are a no-no. The chemical glue will screw with your already battered nails.
- You can paint your nail, but use a polish you have used before, so you know you won't get a reaction.
- Massage cuticle cream into the nail area to prevent dryness, splitting, and hangnails. This sounds gross and not something you would admit in public, but if you do get a bit of loose skin, don't pull at it, as you could cause an infection.
- Gently push your cuticles back with a wooden stick.

Have a chat with the nurse or doctor if you think you have developed an infection.

To make you feel better, remember that black nails are a thing, not just for Halloween. If you type black nails into Etsy, you get 1,000+ results. This £15 product caught my eye.

'Black lizard skin detail handmade press on nails. Builder gel on top of matte black gel polish.'

At the time of writing, they had made 154 sales and got 5 out of 5 stars!

Nose Bleeds

(Will she ever stop—not more side effects!)

I don't know about you, but I haven't had a nosebleed since primary school. We all remember sitting in class with cotton wool stuffed in each nostril. According to every source on the internet, nosebleeds are common between the ages of three and ten. More surprisingly, it's caused by dry air—I didn't know that was a thing. When I had mine, I remember enjoying being the centre of attention and getting out of schoolwork. My mum was brilliant at getting the bloodstains out of my school uniform. For all budding serial killers out there, my mum told me white wine vinegar did the trick.

The further along you get with chemo, an unfortunate side effect is nosebleeds, and they can come as a bit of a shock. I was cooking and suddenly noticed a blood trail across the kitchen floor. I'm not going to lie; it's a shock. I hadn't had one since I was about six and had no idea how to stem the volcano eruption of larva-like blood streaming down my face. To be honest, I'm being melodramatic. It just feels like you need a quick blood transfusion. But don't worry if you do find that you start gushing claret, there are tried and tested steps to follow.

How do you stop a nosebleed?

Tilt your head forward, and with your thumb and forefinger, pinch your nose just above the nostrils. The advice is to breathe through your mouth, but I would say that is bleeding obvious, if you pardon the pun. It usually takes 10-15 minutes to stop, but that can feel like an age when you're crouched over, staring at the bright red, screwed-up tea towel you grabbed in a panic. By the next one, you will be an expert, but if they carry on or you are worried, tell your nurse.

Veins and Phlebitis

I had no idea how stressful this would be for me, but as a result of chemotherapy, I developed phlebitis, an inflammation of the vein caused by inserting the needle for your chemo infusion. The veins are weakened by the drugs and harden up. Every visit will be spent taking fifteen minutes to locate a vein. It's stressful for everyone involved, and the nurses feel terrible. You have to remind yourself they are not trying to hurt you.

You not only have to be injected on chemo day, but you also have regular blood tests at your GP surgery. I nearly had a fit when the usual phlebotomist wasn't there, and the trainee told me she would be dealing with me today.

No offence to less experienced staff, but I cringed when she used words like your veins are being a bit 'naughty.' They are not being naughty; they are being full on serial killers. Unsurprisingly, after several attempts, she had to get a doctor trained in butterfly needles. Don't be fooled by the name; they still hurt.

You can do things to encourage the veins. Drinking lots of water and walking fast to your appointment can help increase blood flow. Once, on the cancer ward, I was given a bowl of water to soak my arm in as they thought this deluded idea would help push my veins to the surface. I ended up spilling it into my lap and sitting with a soaking crotch all the way through treatment. By the time I walked to the car, it looked like I was incontinent.

Once you know they are looking for a vein, anybody will tell you your anxiety soars. You also notice which nurses are on duty and get to know those that, let's say, are less able than others. I know they have to practise, and I know an orange isn't the same as real people, but can't they practise on people who don't have phlebitis?

After my nurse friend's intervention, I was eventually given a port or PICC line. I'm not knocking the NHS, but I think phlebitis is an awful side effect and needs more awareness given to the psychological effects on the patient.

I did some research in some medical journals, so you don't have to.

> [16] *'When trying to identify a suitable scale to assess the severity of chemotherapy-induced phlebitis, it became evident that, despite the existence of a variety of scoring and assessment tools, there is, as yet, no existing phlebitis assessment scale which specifically and comprehensively measures the effect of chemical phlebitis as a result of peripheral chemotherapy infusions.'*

What they are saying, rather pompously, is that they can't measure and compare it to other patients as no one agrees. Surely this needs to be investigated further because it was, without exception, the most stressful element of my treatment.

PICC lines or ports allow the medication to be pumped directly into a plastic tube, bypassing the trauma of the nurse trying to find a vein. Of course, like any procedure, they carry risks and can get infected, but they made my life so much easier.

It seems in the USA, they are offered almost straight away. The fact that I had mine late suggests that it's an issue of NHS funding. Aunty Pyjamas was my PICC line advocate; without her, I am sure I wouldn't have had one. Having said that, when you have your blood tested at the local GP surgery, the nurse may not be trained in PICC lines, so the whole sorry circus of finding a vein happens again. It's not personal; I know the nurses tried their best, and it is also stressful for them.

*Chemo Brain or Chemo Fog?

'Of all the things I've lost, I miss my mind the most.'

~ Ozzy Osbourne

Again, I think having chemo is like being pregnant. Your head turns to mush, affecting your ability to perform the simplest tasks. Let's put that into technobabble talk.

> [17] *'Chemo brain been defined as subtle but persistent cognitive dysfunction frequently experienced during or post-chemotherapy with difficulties relating to maintaining attention, memory, and perceived mental slowness.'*

Sounds like a typical day for me. We all walk upstairs and forget why we are there. Who doesn't mix up their children's names or walk to Tesco for milk and return with aubergine pickle? Or is that just me?

Everyone living in this stress-induced world experiences some form of forgetfulness. However, chemo brain is a little bit more. I ferociously tried to avoid it at all costs. People advise you to keep the mind active with crosswords and sudoku, but I hate puzzles. I attempted to write a novel, and even though I only wrote 200 words a day, it helped keep my mind active. In a way, that was my sudoku.

For me, chemo brain manifested itself as an inability to remember the name of things as simple as ketchup. "Please pass the er…er…the red stuff in the bottle." Not being able to name condiments is the least of your worries. Some people find it affects their ability to cope with the simplest of tasks.

You can do several things that should help you cope better with these changes. Stop doing things that require a lot of mental clarity. It's probably not a good time to assemble an Ikea bookcase or attempt brain surgery. (Not sure which is the more difficult of the two.) If you have any meetings with medical staff, make notes and write things down. Even better, take someone with you to ask the questions and remember what was said.

Make lists! I always used to rebel against my mother's insistence to write a list, but I have to hand it to her, it did help.

Chemo brain passes after 6-8 months, but for some, it can last a lot longer. The most important advice, as always, from your resident lollipop lady, is don't beat yourself up and talk to your nurse.

Things Chemo Can Make You Do

The stress of treatment can affect you in many ways. I used to channel my inner-creative chimp. This is my Lolly Pop Greyson Perry art club entry—a lollypop mini-me made from a bottle of Tesco bleach (as people talk of chemo as bleach) with a table tennis bat as a head. The stop sign is the bottle lid, and the face is an inside-out rubber glove. Surprisingly, it never got featured.

Plonked on the windowsill, it has been, rather poetically, bleached by the sun and is now a poor imitation of its former glory. Joking aside, I found drawing rather cathartic and being creative kept me occupied during the enforced isolation of chemo and lockdown.

Bone Pain

This was one of the most challenging parts of chemo treatment for me. I felt at times like my legs had a twenty-stone weight tied to each of them, and all I could do was lug them from my bed to the toilet. This creeps up on you incrementally, and by the end of your treatment, you feel battered and are counting the days down until your final infusion.

I went to a concert to see *Dead South** halfway through my treatment. Surrounded by my protective entourage, I managed to stand all the way through it and forgot about the leg weight. The worst thing was the toilets didn't have any soap, but the upside was that I made lots of cool young friends who borrowed my hand sanitiser. As they were all slightly worse for wear, they had no inhibitions and asked me about my bald head, and I was very happy to share my story. I felt like a normal person for the first time in a long time.

Neutropenia (or Quadrophenia, As I Like to Call It)

You will have had it drilled into you by your chemo nurse to be vigilant against infection and monitor your temperature. I advise you to do as you are told and not become nonchalant.

When having chemo, we know it can affect every cell in your body. It is not unusual to have a mid-treatment hospital admission. That's why you must monitor your temperature and be careful about any infections. My admission happened because I had neutropenia or, in layman's terms, my white blood count dropped very low. This makes you very susceptible to infection, and you don't need me to tell you why that is dangerous.

When I was admitted, it was a ***Sunday** night and all day my eyelids had been stuck together, and tears were running down my face. I had numerous eye problems while on chemo, so I ignored it. The girls had a party, and I was trying to get everything ready for school. Looking in the mirror, I noticed a rash, but I dismissed it. It wasn't until 10:30 p.m. that I began to notice how hot I was. I eventually took my temperature, and it was 38°. I still didn't think it was a big deal and reluctantly rang the chemo emergency line. The operator insisted that I go to hospital.

Everyone except me had had a drink, so we ended up getting a taxi. £25 lighter, we eventually got to the ward just before midnight. Using our phones as torches, we worked out how to ring the out-of-hours bell. I was whisked into a bed and endured the usual drama of them trying to get a cannula in so I could be pumped full of antibiotics. As I couldn't sleep, I looked around and met the other people in my ward.

They fill you with antibiotics to prevent sepsis. When the nurse told me this, I nearly fainted. It is a precaution, and you are definitely in the right place. While they rushed to get me to the ward, the initial fear turned to relief as I was where I needed to be.

Now, this might make me a bit of a weirdo, but I enjoyed my enforced stay, despite being next to a lady who kept shouting, "Nurse, I'm s***ting myself." All night. Thankfully, she was moved the next morning.

Everyone in the ward had some form of cancer and had reacted to their medication. It is very common, and if it happens to you, remember they have seen it all before. We got to know each other very well. There was an Italian lady who danced down the ward with her walking stick and another lady who made me laugh continually. We were a jolly crew, and in it together, there was a genuine camaraderie. By now, a hardened patient, I had been through a lot, and sort of knew what to expect.

When the doctor did their rounds with their gaggle of ***students** in tow, I modelled my rash like I was on a catwalk. One particularly gormless student sneezed by my bed, and I asked her to move away as I was neutropenic. She looked shocked, and I was amazed at how daring I had been. As I said, I was an old-hand and neutropenic, for God's sake. This was something I would never have done before.

The enforced stay made me feel safe, knowing I was being monitored and in the best environment. It also gave me a break. When you have cancer, you try to keep everything normal, but being in hospital meant I didn't have to worry about the washing, cooking or kids. Sad as it might sound, I enjoyed being around people who understood and could laugh with. The loneliness of treatment is hard and being with them made it feel like a little holiday.

Following my next chemo infusion, they lowered the dose as I was told my admission was 'significant'. This throws up lots of concerns that it won't work, but they assured me they quite often change the dosage as it is not an exact art.

My advice is to make sure you regularly check your temperature and call the emergency line if you have any concerns. If you do find yourself plonked in a ward, tell yourself hundreds of us have been there before, and you couldn't be in a better place.

Hang on in there. Before you know it, you can ring the bell.

The End Of Chemo Treatment

The Bell

At the end of your chemo, you get to ring the bell. It's symbolic of the end of this particular part of your journey. Everybody claps and cheers and I have seen remarkable women on the internet come to their last treatment in ballgowns and shimmering dresses, ready for their photo opportunity. I wish I had thought of that, but I don't own a ball gown.

When it was my time, they had forgotten to give me my Herceptin injection, and I had to hang around and wait for it to come up from the pharmacy. When it did, it was about 7 p.m., and everyone, apart from the cleaners and my nurse, had gone home. So by the time I finally rang it, it was a total non-event and a bit of a damp squib. To be honest, I felt a bit of a fool, but I did it anyway.

Radiotherapy

Another bump in the road might be radiotherapy. If you have had chemo, they will give you time to let your body recover.

After the relative chaos and volume of people having chemo, radiotherapy is a completely different experience. Finally, you get the high-tech gleaming ***intergalactic spaceship**. The bright yellow signs saying, 'radiation-controlled area' and 'do not enter' gives an air of ***Area 51**. The technology is imposing and feels alienesque, but with a machine costing 1.3 million quid, it's probably cheaper to go into space.

Gleaming and impressive, the radiotherapy machine dwarfs you. At the initial meeting, you will be asked to strip off, something you'd expect to be used to by now, but I never was. It's a far cry from the bustle of having chemo, as you are the only patient. Instructed to lie on the chair/couch, you are met by a fresh-faced, and in my case, male technician.

Initially, you will have two technicians, but don't expect to see the same person twice. They talk you through the process and align the machine. Precision is ensured by giving you tiny tattoos to target the right area. I was excited about my tattoo, but it is so ridiculously small that even to this day, I haven't been able to see them again.

As an asthma sufferer, I was checked to see if I could hold my breath. This test shows when your lungs are inflated how much they push away from your heart protecting it from the effects of radiation. I failed the breath tests miserably, so they resorted to plan B. This involved putting a shield across my chest. Once they tinkered about getting the measurements and laying me in various positions, they gave me my timetable of treatments. Mine was every day for two weeks.

Finally, the day arrived, and I drove to the hospital with trepidation. After stripping off, I gingerly laid down while they tinkered with the machine and moved my arms about. They then retreated behind the protective wall while the treatment started, and I closed my eyes.

It's a lonely experience as the machine moves rhythmically across your body. Like with all my treatments, I cried the first time. It's not that it hurts; it's just intimidating. Inside, you feel like a 1960s NASA monkey circumventing Earth while furiously smoking twenty fags. Like those unfortunate chimps, you're heavily scrutinized while having no idea what is going on behind the technology.

Having radiotherapy is like a grown-up game of Sleeping Lions. Told not to move, you wish you could move some part of your body, which is cramping, or scratch something that itches. The more you tell yourself to keep still, the worse it is.

I had fourteen treatments, including one on my birthday, which I remember being particularly peeved about. While it can make you tired, it's not as bad as chemo, and I drove to and from all my appointments which was liberating, as I found it horrendous to rely on lifts. Driving also allows you to stop for cake on the way home. Having said that, there are possible side effects.

Tiredness

This can hit you at any time, even months afterwards. You are so used to feeling below par that it can take you by surprise. It affects everyone differently, and some sail through while others struggle.

Skin

Unsurprising, you can develop a rash. Let's face it, it's hardly surprising, given that you're being bombarded with radiation. You need to be gentle with your skin.

I was advised to moisturise my skin daily. They tell you to avoid creams that contain sodium lauryl sulphate as this is an irritant. Believe me, it's in everything and is the active ingredient that makes your soap froth—yet another thing to feel depressed about, as this is one of the joys of having a shower. I was advised to use E45 cream, but I settled for Aveno. It does, however, cost an arm and a leg, so search for alternatives. There are plenty of creams out there. It's about finding the right one for you and your pocket.

Get out your light floaty clothes, and don't wear anything that will scratch you. I had a rather fetching Afghan dress and floated around like Demis Roussos. Not always practical, especially if it's snowing outside. I wore mine around the house like a '70s extra from Abigail's Party. You are also told not to starch your collar, but if you're anything like me, you are not even sure how to do that anyway.

Be careful not to scold yourself with a super-hot shower or bath. Ice packs and heat pads are also out. If you get a burn, ask your nurse how best to treat it rather than slapping on a plaster, as it's not a good idea to put anything sticky on your skin.

The sun is not your friend. This, unfortunately, is ongoing and gone are the days of smothering yourself in factor twelve and sizzling on the beach. You still need to watch the sun as the skin can become sore if you get burnt. I wore ***sun-resistant clothing** and a scarf around my neck as I was zapped there too. The best advice is to keep out of the sun. As you will discover later in this book, if you develop lymphoedema, being aware of what you wear will become second nature.

Skin Burn

If you react to the radiation, you can develop quite a sore burn. Try not to Google this, as it will freak you out. I was fortunate in that I didn't have any major problems. You will be offered appointments with a nurse who monitors your skin and advises you on how to deal with it. Don't put moisturiser on the burn; you are just asking for trouble. If in doubt, ask.

Sore Throat

If they are zapping you around the collarbone, it can give you a sore throat. I don't remember anyone telling me this, but I had become brave enough by this stage to Google the symptom.

Radiotherapy is exhausting because it's so relentless, but it is less onerous than chemo. Just get on the 'bus'; before you know it, it's over. You also get to ring the bell again, even if you've had chemo.

Like all treatment, this phase will end. The problem is that it does feel never-ending. I had radiotherapy every day for two weeks except Sundays. Not only does the drive to the hospital wear you out, but you have to find the money for petrol, parking and cakes for the journey home. I believe in treating yourself, so don't beat yourself up. It's tough—another big bump in the road but another destination ticked off on your roadmap back to health.

Lymphoedema

If you have had all your lymph nodes removed, you will be at risk of lymphoedema. I don't know about you, but the word lymphoedema is horrendous and sounds seriously wrong. Me being me, I went into super-panic mode.

In layman's terms, it's a build-up of lymph fluid. Without going into some massive medical explanation, your lymph system, which removes bacteria and keeps you healthy, is struggling. The fluid can't move around so easily, which leads to swelling. If you have had surgery that messes with your lymph nodes, you might be susceptible to it. You usually get it in your arm, hand, or body.

I noticed mine when I was eating a sandwich. My left arm seemed particularly puffy with sausage fingers, and there was a ridge of skin across the back of my hand. After a quick visit to the GP, I was referred to the lymphoedema clinic.

The skin feels tight and you can feel the pressure. A bit like the first time you ever tried to get into a wetsuit or even a pair of slightly small jeans. My experience was that it wasn't painful but was uncomfortable.

The main issue is that it can get infected (see the section on '*Cellulitis*'). Jewellery can seem tight, and your arm can ache and feel restricted. I thought cording was bad enough. For me, it happened about five months after surgery, but it can happen much earlier or later. I had all my lymph nodes removed, so I was in the most at-risk category.

So that is the bad news. What can you do about it?

As I write this, it's snowing outside, but I remember insects being the bane of my life. They were difficult to manage, so I have given advice about them in their own section. Mosquitoes and midges are bastards. You don't feel them on your skin, and before you know it, they have chewed half of your arm off. It takes a catastrophic amount of willpower not to scratch frantically, but that can break the skin, allowing infection to breed.

- Wear light-coloured clothing. Insect 'goths' are attracted to dark clothing.
- They also come out early morning and after sunset, so try to walk dogs at different times.
- Wear insect repellent. Although I am your lollipop lady, I am also an ***Avon lady** and cannot recommend 'Skin So Soft' spray oil enough. If you are a mountaineer or a member of the Royal Marines, you'll know it is a well-known insect repellent. I'm assuming

you're not, but it has been shown to offer protection. Some studies say you need a repellent with DEET, but then you have to consider putting harsh chemicals on your skin. Yes, we are between a rock and a hard place.

- Wear insect-repellent clothing. You will have to search for this, and some of the clothing looks normal. I also looked at a full-body mesh suit, which you wouldn't want to wear when you pick up a pint of milk at your local Tesco. However, if you are a hermit and live in a cave, they might be an option.
- Avoid water where insects congregate. Probably best to avoid rivers, and you might find the water butt in your garden is a breeding ground.
- Something that sounds very American is investing in an ***electrical bug catcher**. I haven't done this myself, but they might be worth a try.
- Disinfect any bites at once. If you are unfortunate enough to get bitten, clean it with some wipes. Get in the habit of carrying them in your bag, so you're always prepared.
- Watch out for heat and redness—the tell-tale signs of infection and your cue to see a doctor immediately.
- Remember not to let fear of insects overwhelm you. I put this last one in because I am spectacular at being melodramatic. If you want to sit outside with a gin and

tonic to watch the sunrise, my advice is to do it but follow the suggestions above.

Other things to be aware of:

Heavy weights – It's easy to forget but try not to pick up things that weigh a ton. Not as easy as you might think. You have to do the shopping, kids jump on you when you least expect it, and the dog might yank on your arm. My advice is just to do your best.

Be careful in the kitchen. I now grate cheese in my mini-whizzer machine and carefully cut vegetables. You need to try and avoid any unnecessary cuts.

Also, get some good washing-up gloves and always use them. Your nails will thank you, and the hot water won't aggravate your skin. I bought myself a pair of heavy-duty black rubber gloves, also known as 'Mum's Murderer Gloves', in my house as I look like I am about to dissect a corpse.

Watch the oven, as we all know how easy it is to get burnt. I bought a pair of silicone gloves but instantly lost them.

It's easy to forget, but don't let it rule your life; be sensible. You will cut yourself at some stage. Just clean it and watch for infection, and you'll be fine.

My Experience at the Lymphoedema Clinic

You will be met by a specialist nurse who will measure your arms and compare them. You might think they have some fancy machine to do this, but they simply use a tape measure and a marker pen and measure your arm in centimetre-spaced dots.

Depending on the severity of your swelling, you might be offered a compression sleeve. They are rolled up over your arm so that the constant pressure will help the movement of lymph fluid. It resembles a ghastly pair of American tan tights, but the foot's been cut off.

For my sausage fingers, I was also offered a fingerless glove. Resembling ***Steptoe**, I preferred to call it my gauntlet. Again, it's the same awful colour, and you are advised to wear it when your lymphoedema flares up. However, I found myself forgetting to take it off when I put my hands in water.

There is good news. You can buy funky-designed compression sleeves on the internet that are much cheaper than getting a real tattooed sleeve. A word of warning—you must ensure they fit correctly because an ill-fitting sleeve can worsen your lymphoedema. Also, don't put moisturizer on before wearing your sleeve, as it can damage the material.

The clinic will see you regularly and monitor you. They also give you a series of exercises to help move the fluid along.

Lymphoedema Exercises

The thing about lymphoedema exercises is that you will die of boredom doing them. It's not like you put on Lycra and start excessively sweating while accompanied by pumping music and a personal trainer shouting, "Come on. You smashed it."

You sit quietly and gently stroke your skin in a prescriptive way to drain the excess fluid. You must follow the same steps every time, and it feels like you are doing nothing. It's like watching paint dry or sitting through a two-hour episode of Midsomer Murders with my mother. The exercises are so gentle and dull that you wonder what is the point of doing them. Maybe that's just me, but I am impossibly impatient. What with getting the kids up, cleaning the house, making a living, and generally trying to have a life, is it any surprise monotonous exercises get left behind?

So what is the answer? At the risk of sounding like a schoolmistress, it's routine. You have to commit to doing them at the same time every day, and you have to build them as a habit. But we all know some habits are easier than others, especially if they involve red wine and cooking.

To help me over my mental block, and with the help of my children, I made a joke exercise video. Complete with '80s leg warmers, I channelled my inner Jane Fonda and recorded it on my phone. Playing it every morning and hearing yourself repeat the actions, it soon gets it into your head, and before you know it, it's over.

To my shame, I nearly got kicked out of the lymphoedema clinic for non-compliance, having lost my sleeve and glove twice. It was the necessary nudge I needed. As always, I cried, which I always do when I see a nurse in uniform. Once I had been told off, the nurse discreetly told me her doctor chastised her for not doing her hip exercises. Intellectually, you know you need to do it, but being dismissive as you struggle, is normal.

However, I know someone who religiously does her exercises each day and has made it part of her routine. She sometimes takes before and after pictures and can see what improvement there is after just ten minutes.

It's tough to do exercises and find the time and motivation, so stop beating yourself up. The good thing is they are easy, you can do them anywhere, and they don't make you sweaty. Just get into a routine because prevention is better than cure.

Other Side Effects

Friends and Radio Silence

Most people I have spoken to have had varied experiences regarding friends and the support they were given. Some came out of the woodwork and were fantastic. My friend Anne called me every day and took me to the end of the road for cake and cheesecake at least once a month despite living an hour away. Other people you might expect to rally around drop off the radar and you may not hear from them for months, if at all. This can be extremely unsettling, and you start questioning whether they were fair-weather friends.

Lisa's story

Lisa talked about her experience with someone she had been friends with for years.

'Both of our first experiences with breast cancer were in high school. We had two teachers who were diagnosed, and one of them passed away. But the entire school, at that point, started charity

running. I don't know if you're familiar with Susan G. Coleman's Race for the Cure, but it's a big organisation here. It was at one of these where my best friend and I ran our first race together.

When I was diagnosed with breast cancer, I announced it on Facebook. I asked people through email and Facebook if they wanted to be on a special email list of updates. I knew my best friend was definitely on Facebook, but she did not respond. But I put her on the list regardless.

After I spent the entire year writing to the people on the list, telling them what was going on, she had still not said a word to me about my diagnosis—not a single word. So I thought, okay, well, maybe the email address was wrong or something like that. But when I sent my very last update to them on the list, which was the anniversary of my diagnosis, she responded. I have not responded to her yet because what am I supposed to say? Where have you been?

We fell out of touch for roughly a year. We didn't talk anymore. We only texted, which is so bizarre.

Eventually, she apologised and said she was embarrassed for not contacting me when I was diagnosed. But even then, she would only text every three or four weeks, asking how I was and that she was thinking of me. She sent me gift baskets made by her friend in

Chicago that she went to college with. So she had her friend make and bring me food!

I began to think about how would I want to end this relationship if I was dying. Should I turn the other cheek and respond very politely? But I was angry, so I emailed another friend and asked her for her opinion. She said I could totally ignore it or respond kindly.

I need to decide if I want her in my life moving forward. But I don't think there would be much of a difference if she was or wasn't.'

Lisa's experience shows the emotions you experience when your best friend ignores you. You are left with anger and painful decisions about what to do with that emotion. Cutting people out of your life is difficult and is another burden.

The overriding emotion this perceived abandonment leaves you with is anger. This happened to me with a friend I had known for over twenty-five years. I passive-aggressively made sure she got the message that I thought she hadn't been supportive by telling another friend, knowing it would filter its way down to her. She was horrified and called me, but I let the answering machine pick up the call. I couldn't face speaking to her.

Eventually, I was driving back from the station when she called for the tenth time. I pulled the car over and blurted out how I felt. She was stunned and apologised. Her excuse was that we lived opposite ends of the country, and we didn't ordinarily phone each other every week. I reminded her these were not 'ordinary' circumstances. Holding on to anger is unhealthy, so I felt better for telling her how I felt. We are back to our pre-cancer level of friendship now.

Before, I don't think I would have had the courage to confront her, but having cancer and treatment does harden you and builds resilience whether you feel like a warrior or not. Sometimes you have to do some friendship house cleaning. In many ways, cancer does that for you and separates those you know you can rely on and those that are better ditched. It's a decision only you can make. It's hard to make sense of feeling let down, and it leaves you wondering why people ignore you when you need them the most.

> [18] *'There are a few reasons for this abandonment. It varies, but your friends may not be able to deal with their helplessness in the situation and feel guilty that they can't cure or comfort you. Survivors' guilt, or even relief that it didn't happen to them, can also get in the way. You may find your friends either want to avoid the subject of cancer entirely and go on like nothing is wrong, or they only want to talk about their feelings about your cancer. You are more than your cancer diagnosis, but right now, it's a major part of your life that can't be ignored.'*

Whatever the reasons for their neglect, it can leave you smarting. On the plus side, plenty of people come into your life, and it can be life-affirming when they pop round with cake, take you to treatments or help you choose a wig. Cancer clarifies who your true friends are and who has a good heart. Complex friendships are an unfortunate side effect of cancer treatment, but 'stay on the bus'.

Loneliness

With some friends not being there for you, one of the worst things about cancer is the isolation—the hours spent on your own while the world spins around you at a hundred miles an hour. Some studies suggest loneliness is as bad as smoking fifteen cigarettes a day. Admitting you feel lonely is hard to do. As I write this, I feel a sharp pang of embarrassment. But loneliness was one of the main emotions I felt for long periods of my treatment.

Some of the most amazing songs have been written about loneliness. Roy Orbison, The Beatles, The Police and David Bowie, so you are in good company. Loneliness can mean different things to different people. Most of us, when we were teenagers, have all experienced being on the periphery of a group at school and trying to fit in, feeling invisible. Likewise, when you first leave home, being on your own could feel overwhelming. With time, you improve your social skills and realise the super-cool mean girls at school are all ghastly, and you'd rather not be their friend anyway. That's normal. That's growing up. Likewise, the years I spent working with people with learning disabilities who only had a few people in their lives who weren't paid to be there. Their social interactions were few and far between as the general public tends to shy away from people that are different.

The first time you go out wearing your chemo cap or wig, you feel people looking at you. It's all very well to say sod them and style it out, but sometimes you want to melt into the background. I was once called a weirdo by a woman in Poundland. Taken aback, I just looked back meekly. While lying in bed that night, I came up with lots of witty replies.

When I was diagnosed with cancer, I had just left a very busy job where I scooted around the country and worked with many colleagues. Some were great, others not so, but there was human interaction. Setting up a business with my partner was exciting and scary, but my social circle shrank as we spent all our time together.

Suddenly, my social circle dissolved even more. Diagnosis is shocking, but when you feel ready, you reach out to people, but if your friends and family live a long way away, you can find yourself alone for long periods. The kids are at school, and your partner is trying to earn a living while you can't.

After several chemo treatments, I became increasingly tired and could only really manage a quick walk to McDonald's for a coffee at the end of my road. I liked it there because the cleaner, Shirley, used to come and talk to me. The place was immaculately clean, which, when you are in germ paranoia mode, was a perfect place to be.

There are cancer groups you can go to. That's fine if you live near them, but the closest ones to me were a good half-hour drive away. It felt like a mountain to climb, and I didn't have the energy or confidence. When you are feeling lonely, you forget how to interact. It's easier to go to bed, put a pillow over your head and sleep.

Support Groups

Some people find the various breast cancer support groups invaluable, and I am sure I would have gone to one if it had been around the corner. Of course, they are not for everyone, but I know they are a place you can take your wig off with people who understand and have been through it. They are supportive, and you can be yourself.

To find one in your area, go to the Macmillan website. The link is in the '*Helpful Links*' section.

Of course, there are other local groups, and your breast cancer nurse is probably the best person to advise you. They vary in what they offer and size. Some are in community spaces, while some people host them in their houses. While I write this, I wish I had gone to one. Talking about cancer is complex, and when you are with your friends, you just want normality and have a laugh. With all the added pressure of feeling you have to be brave and 'fight it', it's not surprising people withdraw into themselves.

Online Forums / Facebook Groups

Most of the large charities have online support groups you can join. Here you can chat anonymously with other people. I dipped my toes in but found it frightened me as people talked about all sorts of things I hadn't experienced, making me more paranoid. I also prefer meeting people face to face, but that's just me. Post Covid-19, we are all more comfortable online, but during my diagnosis, I couldn't face it. That was probably more about my state of mind than the groups. A lot of people find them a lifeline.

If you are feeling lonely and disconnected, remember that it's hardly surprising. Don't internalise it. Everyone feels lonely sometimes. It's part of the human condition. Try and take little steps towards meeting people. Try a group, and while it's uncomfortable meeting new people, try and go at least once if you can.

I used the time to write a novel. It was something I had always planned to do. Losing myself in the characters and typing on my computer kept me sane and gave me a purpose. Creativity is a great antidote to loneliness but isn't always an option, especially if you feel low.

Withdrawing can also be a form of depression, so keep an eye on yourself and, as always, seek help if you need to. There is no shame in recognising that you are depressed. You don't have to be a 'warrior' and all that bullshit. If you need help, get it. Talk to your nurse. You won't be the first, and you won't be the last.

Depression

Yes, exercise can help; we all know getting out and about lifts our mood. But what if even doing that is too much? It's not uncommon for people to experience depression, and just getting out of bed is a major trial, let alone going to the shops.

> [19] *'That's the thing about depression: A human being can survive almost anything, as long as she sees the end in sight. But depression is so insidious, and it compounds daily, that it's impossible to ever see the end.'*

Recognition is the First Step

There are common signs that you are depressed. You might have a few of them or the whole shebang. You need to take 'a helicopter view' as one of my ghastly bosses from the 1980s told me. I know using that phrase might make you want to punch me in the face, but what I'm saying is that when you are feeling low, the hardest step is realising that this isn't normal and you don't have to feel like this.

Signs to look out for

- Finding yourself saying things like "I can't be bothered" or "What's the point?"
- Things you used to look forward to, however small, you can't be bothered with.
- You might go days without brushing your hair or showering. You may find yourself wandering about in your pyjamas for days. I used to do this in my youth, but it's not the same.
- You might find yourself withdrawing from friends. You haven't got the energy to phone people or reply to texts.
- Although you might feel tired all day, once you go to bed, you are wired and can't nod off.

- Sleeping all the time. Some people find going to bed switches them off from the world, and they can't physically drag themselves out of bed.
- Inability to concentrate. (This manifested itself for me as an inability to read a book, let alone work.)
- Food becomes a comfort, and you overeat, or you may find the opposite. You know that snacking won't sustain you, but the thought of cooking defeats you.
- You might become emotional over the slightest things and constantly feel on the edge of bursting into tears.
- Mood swings and anger outbursts over the most ridiculous things
- Feelings of wanting to end it all. This never happened to me, but if you have these thoughts, you need to seek help.

Ignore the people who say you've gone through the hard bit, so you should feel better now. They are not your friends.

What can you do?

It's not like breaking your leg. It doesn't have a timescale and a roadmap for recovery. The brain is a complex thing, and we are all different. Don't go down the spiral of comparing yourself or saying what you should be doing. Ignore anyone who says, "So and so had cancer and is fine now."

You never know what goes on in people's minds, and often, people put on a brave face in public only to collapse at home. It's also easy to say, "Don't beat yourself up." But saying and doing are very different. Remember, this will pass. If you have a good day, celebrate it and talk to your loved ones. Again this isn't always easy. Falling down is not an admission of weakness; it takes strength. You have weathered the storm of cancer, and this is another bump in the road.

The Residue of Shame

I am an ex-social worker and have worked with plenty of people who are depressed. I was overwhelmed when my cancer treatment had finished and went to the doctor because my mood was low. With the kids feeling the wrath of my acid tongue, my outbursts were one of the reasons I decided to seek help. Even with some knowledge of mental health, it is impossible to understand just how debilitating it can be until it happens to you.

If I'm honest, and I'm ashamed to say this, I was embarrassed and saw it as a failure. Now I realise my racing mind berating me was the only enemy. Attitudes to mental health have changed. It's okay to say when you feel vulnerable; that takes courage, but it is necessary. I dragged myself to the doctor and, true to form, burst into tears. My doctor was great, and I was given Sertraline, which sort of wrapped everyone in velvet for a few months. I didn't want to take it forever, but it got me over a bump. Some people don't want to take drugs, and I get that too. We have been poisoned by chemo. I would advocate exercise, mindfulness, and diet changes, but sometimes medication is the only route when you can't even do that. It's not a failure; it's you taking control.

Cognitive Behavioural Treatments (CBT) and Counselling

Instead of drugs, you might be offered therapy. The mental health industry is chronically underfunded, and it is unlikely you would be able to access this on the NHS. While you might need to fund these treatments privately, they can be very beneficial and give you strategies for recognising and managing your mood.

If you are one of those people who are resistant to getting outside help, and we have all been conditioned by years of seeing it as a weakness, maintaining a stiff upper lip and all that nonsense. Let me reassure you by turning yet again to the sage below.

'Over the past three years, I have got a therapist. When I was a kid in England, you would not go to a therapist because they'd think you were crazy. It is OK. You ain't stupid for going to a f****** therapist, but you are stupid not to go if you need them.'

~ Ozzy Osbourne

Trastuzumab/Herceptin

Although it sounds like a Greek superhero, it's a targeted drug used for cancers, and for me, it was because I was HER2-positive. It attaches to the HER2 proteins, so the cancer cells don't grow. I had seventeen treatments spaced out over nearly a year.

Not everyone will have it, and at the hospital, I was told I could have it at home. I was so happy as I wouldn't have the gruelling drive to the ward. Initially, it felt like a massive relief until I realised I would have to clean the bathroom and lounge when the nurse came to do the treatments.

Before your first treatment, they take a baseline of your heart, and you may have to visit another hospital for a scan. If you have ever been pregnant, it's similar but not as exciting. (Except for me, who was told I had identical twins and nearly died of shock!)

A technician will cover you in cold gel and take readings of your heart for about twenty minutes. They can then compare this to see if the Herceptin is safe for your heart. Don't be freaked out by this; it's a precaution to protect you. Heed my warning! Every time I had a heart scan, it was freezing, a massive contrast to the oppressive heat of the chemo ward.

Eventually, the day arrives for your first treatment. They give you a passport in which they record all your treatments. So put it somewhere safe, or you'll be like me, scrabbling around for fifteen minutes trying to find it before you arrive.

The nurse reassuringly washes her hands, lays everything out on a super-sterile tray and then administers the drug as an injection, which takes about two minutes. They don't need to find a vein; they just whack it in your thigh. The initial ***prick** stings, but by now, you will be hard as nails, having endured lots of treatments—it doesn't come close to those. And that's it, except the nurse will sit with you for an hour to check you don't have an adverse reaction. So sit back, have a chat or watch the telly.

My favourite nurse was hilarious, and I fed her vegetable soup as she told me she'd only had a Twix for lunch. I was upset when she left. Unfortunately, with the nature of the service, you never see the same person twice. Other nurses were efficient but struggled to engage in conversation, so I just watched Neighbours while they got on with their work.

Side Effects of Herceptin

If you read the potential side effects of aspirin, they will freak you out. As mentioned above, Herceptin can affect your heart. After every injection, my thigh stung, and I developed a bright red circle like a bull's eye around the injection site, which was the size of my hand. Although it looked alarming, it soon faded after a day. Neurotic, as we all know I am, I recorded it in my Herceptin booklet. This is a record of when you have had the injections and a place to write any side effects. By the time I saw the nurse, I had misplaced it and forgot to tell her. As well as potential heart problems, other symptoms to look out for are:

- Feeling sick
- Headache
- A raised temperature or chills
- Cough
- Rash
- Not being able to sleep
- Feeling dizzy

If you are worried, let your doctor know. Like I said to my nurse, you are so used to feeling below par that it is sometimes hard to identify when something is wrong. My advice is if you have any concerns, raise them. You have to sit with your nurse for an hour, so even if they are not talkative, it should help pass the time.

At the end of your Herceptin treatment, they take another measurement of your heart and compare it to the baseline. Pat yourself on the back as you will have completed another part of the treatment roadmap.

Hormone Blockers

Once you have had chemo, radiotherapy or surgery, depending on the type of cancer you have, you may be offered Tamoxifen or another hormone blocker. The drug blocks estrogen that the tumour (don't like that word) needs to grow. By starving it (like that word), the chance of reoccurrence decreases considerably.

You'll be relieved to know that it involves just remembering to take one tablet a day. Okay, that might be for 5-10 years, but thinking back to when you were diagnosed, being in a position of taking a daily tablet, felt like a dream.

I took it for two years. After this, because of my age and menopausal symptoms, I was put on Letrozole. Whatever hormone blockers you take, you are in for the long haul.

Side Effects of Hormone Blockers

You didn't think it would be that simple, did you? Like all tablets, there is a chance of some side effects. Like I have said before, if you read the leaflet inside a box of *Alka-Seltzer, you would never go to the chemist again. Don't become too obsessed about the effects. The most common ones are hot flashes and night sweats, which, let's face it, you're meant to get with menopause anyway, even if yours was chemically induced by cancer treatment.

My friend Estelle suffered from the nightmare of hot flashes. She was so used to suddenly stripping off that when the Amazon delivery arrived in the middle of winter, she greeted the driver in her bra, only realising when she had shut the door.

My advice is to have a mirror by the door and try not to wear frayed, grey bras, which we all wear for comfort. I am sure the Amazon driver has seen it all before. There is a whole army of menopausal women and those on hormone blockers too. Estelle probably isn't the first and won't be the last.

I am not going to list all the side effects; you know your body. If you get a rash, feel sick or see swelling, seek medical help. The best person to talk to about your worries is your medical team. If you don't get on with the hormone blocker they give you, they may be able to offer something else.

Tsunami of Tablets

If you are anything like me, you will have a cupboard full of drugs: anti-sickness medication, steroids, pills for diarrhoea, pills for constipation, and even a couple of bottles of morphine or two. When I was in the depths of chemo treatment, I was religious about when and how I took them, even rinsing my mouth with chemical mouthwash before I took my inhaler. Infection was a real worry.

Tablet Complacency

Scroll forward three years, and I have become complacent. I now have one tablet to take as a hormone blocker. You'd think I would have nailed taking this regularly, but oh no.

I have to set an alarm on my phone, and I still panic every morning, asking my partner if I took it. The problem is you cannot take it twice, so if I'm not sure, I don't take it. It's got to the point where I put my pills on the other side of the room so I can remember getting up to take them. I have to say out loud, "I am taking my tablet."

I can hear my mother berating me. "You had one job to do." The trouble is taking one pill is easy to forget, or maybe that's just me.

Pillboxes

I know you are screaming at me to get a pillbox. Again, I struggled with this. The plastic one I got from a pound shop was difficult to open, and I lost count of the number of nails I broke opening it. You also have to fill it up regularly, and again, I would forget to do this.

Like most things, this problem can be cured with retail therapy. I decided that the pound shop probably didn't sell the best quality plastic boxes, so I scoured the internet for alternatives.

There is a myriad of alternatives, with the sky being the limit. My favourite is a Judith Leiber Couture gold-coloured crystal pillbox shaped like a dice, retailing at £533.07! *'Be one of the lucky ones to snag our dice-shaped pillboxes in fun colours and stunning handset crystal. Buy in multiples and treat your favourite friends.'*

At that price, Judith, I'm afraid I won't be treating any of my friends. Before you return to the pound shop, have a look at Etsy. You will be amazed at the incredible designs. Some are naff, some are amazing, and there are pages of brilliant individual designs. For fifteen quid, you can get something funky and fun. I like the steampunk octopus design. I'm not saying you need to buy a posh pillbox to take your pills regularly at the right time, but it is a step in the right direction.

Getting Rid of Old Medicines

You cannot tip that bottle of morphine down the loo unless you want the local fish population to be off their heads, and they are having a hard enough time with pollution. You should be able to take unused tablets to your local pharmacy. It seems criminal to throw them away, but even if they haven't been opened, they can't be reused. While raging about this, I came across a charity called Intercare, which recycles medicines for people in rural Africa.

If you have unwanted medication, you can drop them off at GP surgeries that partner with the charity. Make sure you haven't opened them, and they have at least fifteen months left on their expiry date. Mine were a mountain of dust when I discovered this charity, but hopefully, you can spread the word. We are lucky to have the NHS, and much as I baulk at the waste, at least you can donate it to people who need it. Details of the charity can be in the 'Helpful Links' section.

If your local surgery doesn't participate in this scheme, give them a kick.

SECTION 3:

Cutting the Apron Strings

Fear of Reoccurrence

The Sword of Damocles

So you have gotten through your treatment, and they have 'cut the apron strings'. You are pushed out into the world like a newborn lamb, leaving you to navigate the rest of your recovery on your own.

Everyone sees you as cured. You've ticked the box, so you have no reason to be down or fearful. The world moves on, but sometimes it can be hard for you to do that too. Many people, including myself, fear that their cancer might come back.

As my friend Elli said, "For many days, you're fine and then get an ache or pain that wasn't there before. You're so used to feeling ill that you're not sure if this is normal or something worse. You're not sure what you need to worry about."

The structure of nurses and doctors isn't on call anymore, and no matter how great your GP is, they will not have the expertise of your oncology team. I'm not criticising GPs, but the brain is only so big, and you can't specialise in everything.

They will put you back in the system if they feel you have a genuine concern.

Recently, I went to the lymphoedema clinic and sat there for an hour and a half despite registering at the reception, only to be told my appointment was for the following week. During that time, I sat with a group of women who had been called back for a biopsy after their mammograms. I watched as they were taken to the room I had been taken to when I received my results. I watched as some came out crying while others skipped away. The fear was evident, and like all women, they supported each other, but for me, it brought back feelings I had suppressed.

Even writing this book, while cathartic in many ways, still makes me feel wobbly at times. We all wonder if it will come back after we have finished treatment—that's natural. Yearly mammograms are just something we all must endure, and if you talk to anyone who has been through treatment, they don't get easier.

Other times you might bump into someone who tells you their cancer has come back, and yet again, you go down the spiral of what if. Not to mention the constant TV, media coverage, adverts, and the unending stream of charity runs with people dressed in pink tutus.

To compound your fear, people now expect you to be okay. They say unhelpful things about the worst being over, but sometimes you get in a mental rut. Sometimes this can be isolating, and you then worry you're being a drama queen. Don't beat yourself up; this is normal.

If those feelings of worry overwhelm you or become too much, talk to your doctor. You won't be the first, and you won't be the last.

Advice

When you are coming to the end of your treatment roadmap, prepare for what's coming next. Ask questions and remember to write them down before seeing your oncologist. If you are anything like me, your mind goes blank as soon as you see a uniform. Take notes or have someone be your secretary if Covid-19 restrictions allow. As your resident lollipop lady, you need to get on a different 'bus'. Find out the roadmap. No one has a crystal ball, and you can't predict the future, but knowledge is power.

Questions you might want to ask?

- What can I expect in terms of how I should feel?
- What symptoms should I be concerned about?
- What can you do to help recovery?
- Telephone numbers and places to call if you have any worries.

If you are struggling, talk to someone. People find groups a great source of help and support. My friend Lisa said Instagram was a lifeline for her, and she made some incredible enduring friendships.

Yearly Mammograms

Nobody enjoys having their boob squeezed between two plastic sheets by a stranger. It's not a fetish I'm aware of, but once you have had breast cancer, they take on a new significance.

You notice the smell and the colour of the chairs. Even though they try to make it look like a sitting room, it will always look like a ward. Or, if you find yourself at the mobile units, it brings back memories of school, detention and caravan classrooms—normally just as cold.

Then there is the room where you were initially told you have 'suspicious cells.' That room always brings the diagnosis flooding back. Mine had a massive faux leather sofa and was furnished with gaudy 1980 wall hangings. It was the best-furnished room but not the one you want to find yourself in.

After the usual battle with the gown (who designs those things?), you'll be called by the nurse. Having had a mastectomy, I always make the same lame joke that I will only take half the time. They have heard it a million times before but laugh anyway.

You then spend the next couple of days waiting for a phone call. It never gets easier, and many women suffer anxiety around it. Yes, you can reframe it and say it's all about keeping you safe, but the fear doesn't really go away.

Parties to Celebrate Being Cancer Free

Some people have parties to celebrate being cancer-free following treatment and go all out. I'd like to think if Covid-19 hadn't hit, I'd have bought a giant unicorn off eBay, donned a white suit, and streamed the Bee Gees, Staying Alive. Maybe that's something I'll do in future years.

Feeling Your Boobs

Once you have been spat out the other side of treatment, you still have to check your boobs. Now for the pathetic amongst you, this fills you with dread and anxiety. Isn't it enough you've already had the yearly boob-crunching mammogram? Like all unpleasant things, like prunes, it is good for you, and you'll thank yourself once it's done.

I was an absolute baby and couldn't face doing it, but I had to get over myself. Depending on your surgery, this will be different for everyone. Many videos on YouTube and apps show you how to do it. Check out the CoppaFeel charity website. I have to admit to being a bit jealous. I love the name, and they have regular hilarious pictures that pop into my Instagram feed. While they target people pre-diagnosis, the rules still apply even if you have been in the system. Their details are in the *'Helpful Links'* section.

What are you looking for?

Despite having a mastectomy, you still need to check your scar. You are looking for unusual areas of hardness or new lumps. I know having a bloody big bumpy scar isn't usual, but it's *your* normal, and you need to know if it changes.

I have to admit that I hate checking myself. I'm not like my friend Estelle who shouts at people in pubs when they go to the loo to check their boobs while they are in there. It's not all about lumps.

If you check out the charity Know Your Lemons (link in the '*Helpful Links*' section), they break down the various symptoms of breast cancer and liken them, if you hadn't already guessed it, to the shape and feel of lemons. The genius of the picture on their home page demonstrates symptoms that most of us are oblivious to.

Estelle went a step further and made a video demonstrating what to look for using real lemons as props. You'll never ask for a slice of lemon in your gin and tonic after seeing 'crusty nipple'.

Unfortunately, it's just one of those things you will have to deal with. Not everyone is as enthusiastic as Estelle, and if it makes you feel any better, I still struggle. Remember to check your armpits and collar bone too. It's not all about the boobs.

The charity Coppafeel has excellent information on how to check yourself and find what is normal for you. So draw the curtains, take a deep breath and make it a regular monthly thing. Also, get all your female friends and relatives to do the same.

Long Term Effects

Bone Thinning and Risk of Osteopenia or Osteoporosis

Having drunk rather a lot of red wine in a noodle bar, I slipped in the bathroom and broke my ankle in three places. Having annoyed my sister-in-law, who I phoned at 11.30 p.m. to take me to the hospital. Don't ask me how I managed to get down the stairs. I waited the obligatory six hours in A & E. I then found myself in hospital for two weeks and immobilized for months. While being diagnosed, I had to answer lots of probing questions about whether or not I was alcohol dependent. I had trouble answering that.

The bad news, and something we have to be aware of, is that cancer treatment can lead to osteoporosis or bone thinning. All women are at risk of this, especially after menopause, so you are not special. The trouble is chemo, and some drugs that block hormones, can lead to an accelerated risk because your estrogen stores have been depleted. Estrogen helps to keep your bones healthy and strong.

After two plates were inserted and eleven screws, I returned home with a zimmer frame and commode. My ankle looked like a gigantic salami sausage, which I had to hide from the dog. I put it down to an awkward fall and bad luck and never gave the cause of the injury another thought. Months later, I had my check-up with my oncologist. Guessing something might be wrong, she rushed through a bone density scan. I already had one ordered, but due to Covid-19 restrictions, this was delayed by six months. I saw the oncologist, and a letter popped through my letterbox the next day.

The rapidity of the appointment suddenly made me make the connection. It wasn't that I was tipsy; that didn't help, but the slip on the wet bathroom floor resulting in such a massive break could be due to my bones being damaged by treatment—yet another bump in the road.

The scan day arrived, and I was met by a rather dashing German technician who made me empty my pockets of any metal. Just as I was to go under the machine, I told him I had a Harrington rod in my back. This threw his plan, so he only managed to scan my leg and arm. As I was leaving, I mentioned that the cold weather aggravated my asthma. Trying to contain his frustrated sigh, he asked me if I was on inhalers. Specifically, if any of the inhalers were steroids. I had failed to disclose this, and as he raised his eyebrows, he told me it could skew the scan results. When you have had so much treatment, you tend to forget things that seem trivial.

I was eventually diagnosed with osteopenia—not as bad as osteoporosis. Having osteopenia meant I was put on a green leafy diet and told to take calcium tablets. My children also delighted in asking me how is my osteo- PENIS.

If you are unlucky enough to be diagnosed, there are some things you can do. As usual, they suck the fun out of life.

- Moderate drinking
- Don't smoke
- Exercise especially weight-bearing exercises like walking
- Eat leafy vegetables

Your medical team will advise you on what tablets to take. If you are diagnosed, get over the shock and remember that plenty of people have it as it occurs when you get older. At least we are in the system, and it was picked up. The good news is you can help yourself by doing the things listed above. There are also various Facebook groups you can join for help and support to help you improve your bone density.

Losing Your Stamina

It comes as a shock, but you just can't do what you used to be able to. Often as women, we are the powerhouses of the family. We think nothing of working full-time, doing the lion's share of the housework and walking the dog. Even though your children cried and begged you for the dog and signed a contract stating they would walk it. (Don't get me started.)

I used to approach everything like a steam train. Now when I do things, I set an alarm for twenty minutes and then have a rest. To make myself feel better, I tell myself I have adopted the Italian technique of Pomodoro, twenty minutes on and off for optimum performance. But actually, it's because you feel permanently knackered.

We have to accept that our bodies feel prematurely aged. Maybe we always felt like that, but now we notice. Before, we may have just ignored aches and pains, but now every new twinge reminds you to switch on your paranoid head.

I have also found myself becoming more sensible. Having my recent diagnosis of osteopenia, I found myself rejecting fashion trainers. "Oh, they won't give me much grip in the rain!" Maybe I'm turning into my mother, but I still won't get a handbag with organiser pockets, something I was relentlessly nagged at in my youth when it took me an age to find my purse, keys and bus pass. To be fair, it's not a joke when you have a dog, lymphoedema and osteopenia. If the dog pulls me over, I could end up in the hospital again.

But before you think all is lost and resign yourself to living with your sorry carcass, remember you have been through a LOT. Going through treatment is like going ten rounds with Mike Tyson. It is not surprising we feel more vulnerable but be kind to yourself. You don't just finish treatment, and suddenly you're miraculously fixed, even though other people treat you like you were. Yes, that door is shut but battered as we are, moving forward can feel difficult and, at times, impossible.

Give yourself a break. Drugs that are strong enough to make your hair fall out are going to take down the strongest. My eyelashes have never recovered, and I still have eyes like a lizard. Take a moment and remind yourself when you heard the word cancer. You are a lot further than you thought, so pat yourself on the back for that.

Looking After You

Your body might feel knackered, but you can slowly restore some of your health. We are bombarded by women with flat muscular stomachs lifting weights in spray-on leggings. I also live in a town with a sports university, so I am surrounded by Lycra-clad students jogging at six in the morning when any self-respecting students should be crawling home, having been clubbing all night.

Before you put the pillow back over your head, remember these are not the norm. Take a gander at the average woman wandering around Tesco; we come in all shapes and sizes. If you want to join a class, find one with women like you; there are plenty around. But even that might feel too much for you. Even before I had cancer, I joined a gym and went for all of two sessions, put off by the man next to me on the cycling machine with thighs the size of my torso. It's finding what is right for you.

Types of Exercise You Can Do

For me, walking was my saviour. It's free, and you can just go out of your front door, if you have a dog, even better. An added bonus is I can emotionally blackmail my children over their laziness about taking the dog out.

You are unlikely to get injuries, and most importantly, it's cheap. Just ten minutes of fresh air can have an enormous impact on your overall wellness. When I first started walking, I went out for ten minutes every day. It seemed pathetic as I lumbered to the local park, but I soon built it up to half an hour. When the wind is blowing, and the rain is throwing itself down, you might not feel like it, and neither might the dog. Once you have coaxed the mutt out, it does blow the cobwebs away. If walking doesn't do it, try other things. I hate swimming, can't stand being cold, and am a natural-born sinker, but I'll pop on the Wii and dance like no one is watching to an '80s classic, whatever floats your boat. It has been known for many years that exercise helps your mood, as this fabulously pompous article from the Journal of Clinical Psychiatry says.

> [20] *'Aerobic exercises, including jogging, swimming, cycling, walking, gardening, and dancing, have been proved to reduce anxiety and depression. These improvements in mood are*

> *proposed to be caused by exercise-induced increase in blood circulation to the brain and by an influence on the hypothalamic-pituitary-adrenal (HPA) axis and, thus, on the physiologic reactivity to stress. This physiologic influence is probably mediated by the communication of the HPA axis with several regions of the brain, including the limbic system, which controls motivation and mood; the amygdala, which generates fear in response to stress; and the hippocampus, which plays an important part in memory formation as well as in mood and motivation.'*

I couldn't have put it better myself. Your mind is the most powerful organ in your body. Runners say 99% of endurance comes from your mind. Now I'm not saying you need to run across a desert with a rucksack filled with rocks until your toenails fall off. If you're like me, chemo has already done that to you. The point is you can choose, and I use that word loosely because sometimes all we want to do is curl up in a ball and count the woodchips in the anaglypta wallpaper. But if little by little, you can edge your way towards a healthier lifestyle, even if it is just a shuffle to the end of the road.

Exercise classes for people who have survived cancer are organised in some areas, but if you're not in a major city, it's unlikely you can access them. You might want to check out the Moving Through Cancer website. This is an American initiative to help people use exercise as part of their recovery and after treatment. Their details are in the *'Helpful Links'* section. It has video guides and information, as well as an online community. As your lollipop lady, I will reiterate to check with your team; you don't want to injure yourself.

Mindfulness

At the risk of sounding woo-woo, mindfulness is a great way of feeling better. I'm not talking about meditating for hours until you can levitate. Great if you can, but if you are anything like me, you spend the whole time thinking of the washing you need to do.

Mindfulness can be active. That means you notice the trees, the grass, the puddles, and the moss on the walls. Wherever you are, it makes your brain slow down. There are lots of amazing apps you can download that help you slow down. It takes practice and patience, but it is a great help.

Self-Care

We all soldier on. We are told to be brave, to fight it, and that we are survivors. I have already ranted about this, so let's not go there. But let's not forget that we have been through the mill. We are allowed to feel sorry for ourselves and, God forbid, as women, put ourselves first. Yes, we still need to manage the kids, the house, and everything else we do that is invisible to everyone, but it is important to find time for yourself.

As I write this, I have just had a tantrum because the kids have come in and interrupted Neighbours. It's twenty minutes long—that's right, twenty minutes, and I don't even have time to watch it. I watch it because it's a mindless soap that requires no thinking or intellect on my part. I make no excuses, but we all need time for ourselves. In my household, a long soak and a facial aren't going to happen.

If you Google 'self-care', the internet is similar to competitive mums at the school gate.

Ten self-care ideas. Hang on, this one has forty-five self-care ideas. Oh, actually, the winner so far with 275 self-care ideas is.... It's the usual stuff—take a bath with bubbles/buy flowers/paint your nails etc. They then try and flog you a manicure set, and you find out the article is an advertorial.

They use words like 'nourish'. If you were bought up in the '70s or '80s, self-reliance and getting on with it is your default setting. But you have had cancer. Your body feels like it's been run over. You're scared about the future, never mind the financial hit you've had to endure not being able to work or, worse still, having to fund your health care like our American sisters. So, if you are in the UK, you are lucky.

At the risk of sounding like a '70s hippy, gratitude is a perfect way of feeling better. I start the day lifting my arms and saying, "WA HOO!" At first, I was making fun and doing it ironically, but it does work and makes me laugh out loud. My long-suffering partner stumbles into the bathroom, and while the bath is running, I hear him shouting, "WA HOO!" It's become a bit of a joke in the house, but it makes us laugh, and that's the point.

People suggest keeping a gratitude diary, but my kids found mine and quoted it to me for a week. *"I am grateful I went shopping on Saturday, and tea is already planned."* Much laughter ensued, and then they began making things up. *"Mum is grateful that her kids are so cool."*

Now I record my gratitude in the notes section of my phone. It's physically impossible to be depressed when you are expressing gratitude. In my youth, self-care or self-indulgence would be cracking a can of Stella Artois open and smoking twenty fags, which you still might want to do, but it isn't going to help.

Yoga

Science has shown that yoga can be highly effective in helping with many of the symptoms associated with cancer treatment, including feeling knackered.

> [21] *'Yoga is increasingly recognized as a complementary approach to diminishing the onset and severity of cancer-related symptoms and/or treating such symptoms.'*

The study of complementary therapies for cancer survivors is gaining traction and hopefully will become more mainstream as time goes on.

I worry that the instructors, who always look about twelve, are inexperienced, especially with someone as decrepit as me. I fear that as I have lymphoedema and osteopenia, I might aggravate this condition.

Let's face it, most doctors look like they should still be in school. When I was having my mastectomy, I asked the fresh-faced consultant when he would qualify, only to be told he was the senior doctor on the ward that day. I was too busy bawling to become embarrassed.

There are people out there that specialise in yoga for cancer patients. It's about doing your research. Any concerns you have can be mitigated by your specialist team, and they will likely be able to recommend someone great. While I know I can probably manage the corpse pose, everything else seems out of my league, but nothing ventured, nothing gained. In the future, I plan to explore this avenue more.

Bladder Problems

There I said it aloud. Breast cancer can have you reaching for the TENA Lady pads, and I don't just mean because you laughed. Being bashful, I found this yet another embarrassing side effect of treatment. I included this in cutting the apron strings because this developed later for me but can happen anytime.

Nobody told me chemotherapy could make you more susceptible to bladder problems. These can take many forms.

- Needing to pee more often
- Losing bladder control
- Infection accompanied with a burning sensation when you pee, a temperature, or UTI (urinary tract infection) as chemotherapy lowers your immune system.

I was never told that hormone blockers which affect estrogen levels, such as Tamoxifen, have a knock-on effect, making you need to pee more frequently.

> [22] *'When used for treatment, both Tamoxifen and aromatase inhibitors can lead to vaginal dryness, itching, irritation, painful intercourse, painful urination, or recurrent urinary tract infections. Since many women are unaware of these side effects, they often go left untreated and are instead pushed aside as an afterthought of cancer treatment.'*

What is important here is that they aren't highlighted to women, and with the embarrassment and stiff upper lip, we don't recognise them or seek treatment. It doesn't affect everyone, but many women, me included, find the constant need to pee inconvenient and annoying.

We have all been cosy and wrapped up in bed, only to have to rush to the bathroom. But when this becomes a constant, your bladder becomes an obsession. As my friend commented, *"I do my 10,000 steps just going to the loo at night."*

Yes, this is an unfortunate side effect of ageing, but it is aggravated by chemotherapy. I have, at times, thought twice about going to places because of the lack of public toilets, and I am not alone.

> [23] *'The BBC found that while in 2010, major councils ran 5,159 public toilets, in 2018 they ran only 4,486. Over the last two decades, the number of public facilities in the UK has dropped by 39%, while the population has increased by more than eight million. Since 2010, 60p in every pound local government receives from central government has been cut – and because local authorities are not legally required to provide public toilets, they fall victim to these cuts.'*

Covid-19 has exacerbated this, but now there is an app telling people where they can find toilets. I have detailed it in the *'Helpful Links'* section.

Vaginal Dryness

What a horrible word. I thought I might shorten it to an acronym, but that's VD!

If it was men, you could bet there would be much more fun and less offensive language word you can use. It's much more acceptable for men to talk about their nether regions. However, I remember being traumatized by a 1980s advert for jock itch when I was in Florida.

Vaginal dryness can be the result of chemo, estrogen blockers or menopause. If you would struggle to talk to your pharmacist, check out ***Cosmopolitan's** list of words that people call their vaginas—link in the *'Helpful Links'* section. My personal favourite is fandango.

I'm sitting in McDonald's while I write this and hope none of the teenage boys at the next table will read over my shoulder. Lucky for me, they're too busy punching each other.

In the spirit of 'staying on the bus', let's call it your mojo motor. And like all engines, they need lubricating—yuck, another horrible word.

I sit here contemplating why I'm being so prudish about writing about something that causes a lot of women real problems, not just after chemo but during menopause or, if you're 50-something, probably both.

As women, we shouldn't be embarrassed about our bodies, but here we are. With my feminist rant over, let's talk about symptoms and how they might affect you.

- Itching
- Soreness
- Pain
- The need to pee
- Susceptible to urinary tract infections.

The NHS website says:

[24] *'These things may make you feel less like you want to have sex.'*

Duh, I should bloody think so.

My friend, who chooses to remain anonymous, was diagnosed with terrible thrush and given a mountain of medication. She said that one day she'll open her stacked cupboard and be crushed to death by the number of pessaries she has stored there. She found her symptoms very debilitating. The thrush treatment didn't work, and she had difficulty walking because of the pain. Eventually, she scoured the internet and suggested to her nurse that it might be vaginal dryness. They recommended some cream, and it soon cleared up.

Some health professionals don't always diagnose correctly, and you know your body better than anyone, so tell them if you suspect something else. While you may not have such severe symptoms, it's worth being vigilant. Don't suffer in silence. Talk to your nurse.

My friend recommended MooGoo, Udder Cream, which has a hilarious back story. A woman used it on the udders of her cows in Australia and then tried it on herself and found it miraculous. No, I don't have a share in the company, but my friend raved about it and said her healthcare team recommended it. (Other creams are available.)

Genetic Testing

You think the nightmare of waiting for results is a thing of the past, but you might be offered a genetic test. Depending on your age, the type of cancer, and family history, it will be offered to determine if you carry the BRCA1 and BRCA2 genes. If you haven't guessed, the BRC stands for breast cancer.

What is it?

> [25] *'Some people have a higher risk of developing breast cancer because they have inherited an altered gene. Genetic testing is used to find out whether an altered gene runs in the family. An altered gene may also be referred to as a gene change, fault, variant, or mutation.'*

Let's ditch that word 'mutation'. We are not zombies, and for the sake of 'staying on the bus', we shall call it the much more palatable name of an 'altered gene'.

I went to the appointment on my own. I thought it would just be an information-gathering event; I hadn't considered the implications. My doctor was great and explained why I was there and what genetic testing was. He confused me completely by asking about my mental health. Unlike most hospital treatments, which treat you like a car that needs fixing, this doctor took the time to explain the implications of having the test. He wanted to ensure I was emotionally prepared for the potential fallout.

True to form, I cried and blubbed down the phone to my partner, who had been as oblivious as me. Despite my usual inclination to bury my head in the sand, I had a follow-up appointment and decided to take the BRAC test. The reasoning being that it might help my children and the wider family.

One of the most important things is family history. As always, I rang my mum and asked her to write down our family tree. It's not as much fun as when you're doing it with Ancestry.com, where you find out your relative had syphilis, was a suffragette, and ran off to the circus. (Although, in our family, we were disappointed to only find farm labourers.) Trying to find out who died prematurely and why takes on a more macabre quality.

My mum approached it like an army manoeuvre, no mean feat considering she doesn't use the internet and is quite hard of hearing. But within two days, she had phoned most of the family, compiled an extensive possible candidates list and had everyone's date of birth and death details going back a hundred years.

My dad was one of seven, and each died of cancer, in addition to a close relative who died as a child. When I mentioned how shocked I was, my stoic mother reassured me it probably didn't mean anything as they were all chain smokers and most lived to a ripe old age. I appreciated this, but at the same time, I reverted to a fourteen-year-old, as we always do with parents, and reminded her that everyone thinks they are a bloody cancer expert.

Once I had recovered from my tantrum, I looked at the list, which was quite sobering. It's difficult because records are sparse, and life was a lot harder then than it is now. We didn't have the NHS until 1948, so many people couldn't afford medical help.

For my next appointment, I took my partner and the list prepared by my mother. The test felt like a no-brainer for several reasons. If it was identified, I could be prepared, but more importantly, we could protect our children and qualify them for early testing. Having said that, it was still terrifying to think that the gene might have been passed down to them.

What is the test?

It's a simple blood test. Mind you, with my phlebitis, there is nothing simple about finding a vein in my arm. They send it off to some *laboratory boffins who can determine if you are susceptible. All you can do is wait. As a veteran of breast cancer testing, you think you would be better prepared, but you never are. The results take about 4-8 weeks.

My doctor called me to tell me the good news. As usual, I cried. At the time of writing, I am contemplating further tests that I qualify for due to my family history. My philosophy is if the test will help your kids, then go for it.

What happens if you are positive for the gene?

Finding out you have the BRCA1 or BRCA2 gene may send you into a spiral of anxiety. Once you're over the initial shock, remind yourself that information gives you power. I know this is easier said than done.

There are risk-reducing treatments that your health team will advise you about. The major charities also have excellent information and resources.

You might be asked to consider the following:

- Surgery to remove the breasts
- Surgery to remove the ovaries and fallopian tubes if this has been identified as an inherited risk
- Drug treatment

As always, think of your questions before meeting your health providers and weigh up what is best for you.

Following a trip to the hairdresser with her mum, Holly noticed a poster with the signs and symptoms of ovarian cancer. The information struck a chord with Holly's mum, who went to the doctors and was subsequently confirmed as having ovarian cancer.

This is Holly's story.

The ovarian cancer my mum had picked up the gene – BRCA1. They told her it was hereditary and could run in the family. She thinks it came from my great-grandfather's sister, who had breast cancer. It can affect men as well, of course.

But the decision came whether I should take the test as there was a 50/50 chance that it could have been passed to me. I received lots of information through the post from the NHS about the test, what it means, and to decide if I wanted to know because some people don't, but I thought forewarned is forearmed.

Knowing you have something means you can take the necessary steps to do all you can to keep an eye on it. So I decided to take the test, and several of my other relatives did as well. The results showed I was the only one who had it. Our local hospital was fantastic. They have a breast care team, and they booked me in for an ultrasound, a scan, and a pelvic examination to check my ovaries. I also had a mammogram and a breast MRI. It was also suggested I make an appointment for an ultrasound to check my ovaries.

I met with two people at the hospital, and they went through the options, including whether I wanted to have any preventative surgery. We discussed whether I wanted a mastectomy and the different options regarding reconstruction with implants or DIEP Flap.

I eventually decided to opt for annual mammograms and MRIs and regularly do self-examinations. I have a contact in the breast care team, my liaison person, and she is really good. She's the same lady that dealt with my mum. They are good if I need to discuss anything.

Holly was also given the option to have her ovaries out.

I didn't decide straight away because it's quite a big decision. Particularly if it's preventative and not something you have to do.

Holly said her approach to having the gene was quite pragmatic.

Well, I'm one of those people who is fine and quite chilled about everything until something happens. Even though I have the BRAC1 gene, it's not affecting me yet. So until something happens, my brain doesn't worry. If I allowed myself to think about it, I had some low moments, but those thoughts can spiral. I try to stop them and tell myself not to go there and that everything's fine. There is no point worrying.

Pink Fatigue

I was relieved to read about pink fatigue, and I thought it was just me being a cynical bah humbug about the endless pink fundraising events and products. It seems I am not alone; some people are a little fed up with the pink ribbon, while some women positively hate it.

If you have recently been diagnosed, you probably will consider slamming this book down and refusing to read more. But bear with me. Of course, it has done a lot of good, but no one is safe from the tsunami of pink—men in warehouses donning pink tutus with the obligatory ribbon, corporate companies slapping a ribbon on their product with a percentage going to charity etc., but ultimately, they aim to sell more. To me, it feels dated, reinforcing the cliché that you have to fight it and be a pink warrior while remaining relentlessly cheerful.

In her book *Pink Ribbons, Inc.,* author Samantha King exposes how the breast cancer support industry is a money-spinner where the serious issue and needs of women are ignored. Of course, it's more complex, and you have to weigh up the money needed for research and help. She criticises the Komen Foundation for partnering with KFC, where you could buy a pink bucket of unhealthy chicken. As she said, [26] *"What's next? A pink cigarette for the cure?"* Whatever your view, the pink ribbon is everywhere, and you will not be able to escape its grasp.

My daughter and her aunty did the Race for Life dressed in the obligatory pink leg warmers and tutu. People are encouraged to write about whom they are running for. My sister-in-law went the extra mile and had the name 'Baldy' across her back. This was my affectionate nickname that lost much in translation. I wasn't at the Oscars, I'm no Jada Pinkett Smith, and it didn't offend me. On the contrary, it made me laugh, but she was politely asked to remove it, and I can see why. Not everyone has the same experience or sense of humour, and people process pain at different points. You have to be understanding but being called 'Baldy' and being the butt of a joke made me feel normal. But I get how it might have offended people, especially those who have lost someone recently diagnosed. We all know what a snivelling wreck I was.

My sister-in-law finished the race and promptly had a hip replaced within six months. As she said, it was more of a 'hobble for life'. My daughter ran all the way, got bored waiting for her, and left. By the time she crossed the line, everyone had gone home. But like I said to her when she was moaning, "At least you haven't got cancer!"

Breast Reconstruction

I could have put this section next to mastectomy, but I can only speak from my own experience. As I write this, my breast reconstruction has been delayed by four years because of Covid-19. While I can't tell you what it feels like to have breast reconstruction, I can guide you on the fears and concerns that the procedure has because I've had three long years to think about it and do the research. Let's address the most important worry.

> [27] *'Breast reconstruction does not increase the chance of cancer coming back or developing in the breast. Reconstruction does not make it harder for your doctor to diagnose a possible reoccurrence. They can still check any changes in the breast area.'*

When can you have a reconstruction?

- At the same time as your mastectomy – immediate reconstruction
- Or, as in my case, years later – delayed reconstruction

You may be offered breast reconstruction at the same time as your mastectomy. This was offered to me as a potential option, but because the Plastics Team and the Surgery Department must coordinate, there would have been nearly a month's delay.

As you know, I had surgery within three days of diagnosis and was in no fit state to decide. In retrospect, given some other complications I have, it was the correct cause of action despite being stuck with my heavy prosthetic.

Your surgeon may also decide that immediate reconstruction isn't the best option if you are likely to have other treatments, such as chemotherapy or radiotherapy. They may also do the surgery in stages. While it might seem like a sea of decisions, remember they have seen it all. Have a list of prepared questions, and take someone with you who doesn't stare vacantly at the mouth of the surgeon while nothing registers.

Types of Reconstruction

Nothing is ever simple. Not only do you have to decide if you want reconstruction, but you also need to look at the types of reconstruction available. Ask loads of questions and be guided by your surgeon.

Breast implant

These are the ones we are more familiar with—the old airbags favoured by Hollywood superstars, and you dream of running down the Californian coast in a red swimsuit with perfect, perky breasts followed by a young David Hasselhoff.

It has advantages, and the scarring is not as pronounced with delayed reconstruction. But don't raise your expectations unrealistically. Some women are very happy with the results, while others are disappointed. They do not behave like your previous breast in shape and feel.

If you opt for immediate reconstruction, you will have a longer recovery time. You might bear this in mind if you have difficulty dealing with your cancer diagnosis. Your boobs feel like a secondary consideration, but to some women, they can affect their self-esteem and body image. No judgement here; we are all different.

Tissue taken from another part of your body

There are two main types of this surgery:

- Reconstruction using body tissue from your back (latissimus dorsi or LD flap). Excuse the Latin. It is just a fancy name for the muscle in your back. They use this and the skin to craft a new boob.

Apparently, this is the simpler of the two options to take tissue as it keeps its own blood supply, which means there is less chance of complications.

- Reconstruction using your tummy tissue (TRAM or DIEP flap). Read this quickly because it seems impossible, but the surgeon takes part of the muscle, including skin, fat and blood vessels and creates a new boob.

Like a tummy tuck, you do lose fat on your stomach. Before you crack open the champagne, it is worth remembering that it can make you susceptible to hernias in the future as it weakens the abdominal wall. Let's leave ourselves with the image of a lovely flat stomach, shall we?

Emma had DIEP surgery three years after her mastectomy. She wasn't offered reconstruction at the time of removing her breast due to her overall treatment plan. When she was eventually offered surgery, she gave me an account.

'My surgery was delayed due to the pandemic. The hospital where I had my mastectomy didn't do this type of reconstruction, so I had to go to another hospital with a different surgeon. I was told I would still have to wait due to the backlogs, but I was offered an earlier

surgery appointment with yet another surgeon. I met him, and we discussed what would happen.

On surgery day, a completely different surgeon came to my bedside, which unnerved me. The surgeon who I had discussed everything with had Covid-19. They asked me if I wanted to reschedule, but I still wanted to continue.

After the operation, you are wrapped in a suit that pumps warm air around your body. This is to ensure that the blood keeps pumping through the grafted skin. Having hot flushes while wearing this suit was pretty unbearable, and you have to leave this on for a couple of days.

Once it's removed, you will be seen by the physiotherapist who wants you to start using your stomach muscles immediately—the last thing you want to do. They will make you sit up without any aids, pulling on something, rolling on your side or anything like that. You have to use your stomach muscles alone. They will also make you cough. I was coughing like I had a slight tickle in my throat, but they want you to cough like you're a TB patient!

The recovery took a while, and I underestimated how much my body had gone through. I was tired and pushed myself too early, resulting in an infection. So make sure you do as your doctor says and take it easy.

> *I'm pleased with the results. However, my new body is not what I expected. Your tummy may be a bit flatter, but it looks a different shape which took some getting used to. The scarring is quite extensive, but I don't mind that. I have a pair of boobs now, which is what I wanted.'*

Emma also had surgery on her healthy boob. They lifted it and removed and reattached her nipple to give symmetry and balance to her reconstructed breast.

My Experience

Having had surgery on my back as a child, I know I'm a physical wreck. They decided the best course of action was to use my tummy for the reconstruction. They first check that you have enough (tissue) fat to sculpt your new boobs. My surgeon patted my stomach, looked at the nurse, nodded and said, "Plenty, plenty." Slightly taken aback, I remember thinking, *I am here, you know* and said, "I could have told you that."

If you haven't guessed, they decided my abdomen was the best site for the donor tissue.

Decisions

As I have had a massive delay in waiting for my surgery, I have had a long time to think about it. Part of me wonders whether it's worth it. I have survived for four years being lop-sided, but then we have been in lockdown for a large proportion of that. If I have a meeting, I whack on the old falsie and endure the discomfort for a couple of hours. The thought of going into hospital again, especially as I had an unwelcome two-week stay with my broken ankle, doesn't fill me with joy. At the time of writing, I am erring on the side of having it, but it's another year away, so I might change my mind. Some women decide not to, and there is a whole movement of women who embrace their flat status.

If you are in the camp that has breast reconstruction surgery after your other treatments, there will be lots of procedures and meetings.

Your photoshoot

You are taken to a room where a technician takes photos of you from every angle. I found it a bit intimidating, like I was a piece of meat or starring in a porn film. Ridiculous, I know, but we don't often take our clothes off in front of people. Well, I don't, anyway.

You then have an appointment with the surgeon. I gaily skipped to mine as it was in a private hospital. In my head, I was convinced they would do the procedure there due to Covid-19, and I would get posh hospital food and hotel-standard accommodation. The reality was something different.

I was weighed in a freezing room and taken into another where there was a surgeon and two students. Stripped off, they examined my tummy, lifting rolls of fat and exclaiming amongst themselves, "Look at this subcutaneous fat…look at that…."

Disapprovingly, the surgeon asked me if I knew how overweight I was and how much I weighed. Humiliated, I snapped back. "If you want to know how much I weigh, why don't you ask the nurse? She just weighed me."

As you know, I love the NHS and will go on any march to support it, but sometimes surgeons need to be more sensitive to the patients. I know they need to be direct, but it's bad enough to stand there naked being poked about by strangers without the fat shaming.

Of course, this wasn't his intention. The fat conversation was about my well-being. He needed me to lose weight until it was safe to have the operation, but at the time, all I heard was fat, fat, fat!

When I left the appointment, I had steam coming out of my ears, and by the time I had finished ranting and jabbering, my partner asked me if I wanted to make a complaint. But as I said, "Next time I see him, I'll be unconscious, and he'll have a knife in his hand."

To be fair, the conversation did spur me on to lose weight, and after doing the 5:2 diet religiously, I lost two stone. Of course, I put most of it back on when I broke my ankle and couldn't walk for months, but that's beside the point.

Weight is something you need to be careful of when you have breast cancer as the various drugs can make you balloon, as well as the enforced sedentary lifestyle.

Scan on your tummy

They will also ask you to have a scan to check the blood vessels in your stomach. My scan was delayed, and to deal with the backlog caused by Covid-19, my appointment was at 7.30 p.m. on a Friday. As I had broken my leg, I had to get my good friend to give up her Friday night, and a date, to drive me to the hospital. Late on a Friday night, the ***Outpatient Department** felt like a dystopian horror film; no one was around. I expected zombies to jump out at me as I wandered around, trying to find the right department. Eventually, a nurse took pity on me (or she could have been a spectre), and

I was directed down a myriad of corridors. By now, I was late. I then had to register my attendance on a machine, and I wasn't sure I had done it correctly. I was then anxious that no one knew I was there.

Eventually, I found the right place and was given a cannula, so they could inject a dye to help with imaging. I endured the usual struggle with finding a vein and proceeded to have a stomach scan. I found the whole experience very bizarre. On leaving, my friend and I drove to the pub.

Weeks later, I had a telephone conversation with my surgeon, who said my blood vessels were okay. This time there was no discussion about my subcutaneous fat but just the words that my surgery had been delayed by another year.

By the time you read this, I hope I will have had the surgery, and I will let everyone know how it goes on my social media, so watch this space.

Going flat

I didn't even know it was a potential option. Only after scrolling through Facebook and immersing myself in information about breast cancer surgery did I realise it was a thing. Maybe in the USA, it's more prevalent, but it wasn't even offered as an option to me.

I Googled it and was taken down a very interesting rabbit hole about conspiracy theories by flat earth believers. If you haven't guessed it, that's something else. Lucky for me, I also stumbled across the organisation Not Putting on a Shirt which advocates for women to have the choice to go flat and has several videos and resources.

Going flat after your mastectomy can be a real option, and many women who choose it look amazing. There is a whole movement that advocates the benefits of going flat.

- More surgery could cause complications. At the time of writing, the thought of going back into hospital fills me with dread.
- Some women don't like the idea of implants and see them as unnatural foreign bodies that could later cause complications.
- Don't be pressured into making a decision. You may decide not to decide just yet. At the rate I'm going, I'll be seventy before my surgery, and by then, I may have changed my mind.

Tattoos

On the internet, you will see many women who have chosen to have tattoos to cover their scars post-mastectomy or reconstruction. If the thought of someone sticking needles with permanent ink where you have suffered so much trauma makes you wince, think again.

Keep an open mind. Some tattoos are amazing works of art. The history of tattooing is rich and complex. There is evidence that tattoos have been used in ancient cultures and have spiritual, cultural and creative meanings. They are much more than drunken mistakes on a stag night.

Choosing a design gives women a sense of control and ownership of their bodies. A recent article by Rachel Lubitz captures the power that people feel from choosing a tattoo.

> [28] *'I had my tattoo done on the one-year anniversary of my mastectomy: May 18, 2017. That day held every emotion that I have available to me. We did it in about four hours. During the tattooing process, we talked about how I felt that my body had been mutilated, and had turned into something that was like a traitor*

to me. It was wild to sit in that chair and think that, just a little over a year ago, I didn't see anything coming. Now I have a short, spiky blonde mohawk, new breasts that don't do anything, and I'm getting a huge tattoo. I cried multiple times from the power of it all, and at the end, I tearfully thanked David for giving me a piece of my body back. I really felt that way.'

I toyed with the idea of having one and still might, but I have several concerns. I've researched, so you don't have to.

Will it affect the skin post-radiotherapy or mastectomy?

Stick needles in your skin, and you have to expect redness and discomfort. The initial irritation should improve with time. If, however, it stays and is accompanied by a high temperature, you need to seek medical help. For all of us who have had chemo, we are used to taking our temperature.

When is it safe to do it?

Like my advice throughout this book, talk to your nurse. You should wait about a year to ensure the skin is healed and robust enough.

Your tattoo artist will not inject the actual scar but, instead, make it part of the design. There are thousands of designs, and it's a matter of choice of how much or little you have done. There are sites on Pinterest dedicated to this, so scroll through and take your time.

Will it make your lymphoedema worse?

This, for me, was the most worrying factor. The jury seems to be out on this as some people say absolutely not, while others say it might. Infection, however, following a tattoo isn't going to help.

Charities like Fuck Cancer in the USA will pair people with a tattoo artist. They also raise funds so people can pay for it. The cost of a tattoo will vary depending on its size and design.

The *'Helpful Links'* section has a link to the charity, Nip. They have started a map of tattoo artists skilled at tattooing on nipples.

Lisa's tattoo story

I include Lisa's story because many women on the internet post shots of themselves with their mastectomy scar transformed into beautiful designs. Lisa's story is more unusual as she had a tattoo to cover up her port scar.

'When I was diagnosed, it was not the first thing on my mind, but I noticed that people would sometimes get tattoos if they had had mastectomies. I thought, oh, yeah, I'm definitely going to get a tattoo to cover up the scar where my port line was.

But I noticed that my scars didn't really bother me except for my radiation tattoos because I didn't have a choice. When I was told I would have three little dots on my body and they would be permanent tattoos, I panicked, and it felt like I had lost control. I remember it really hurt, too. So since then, I knew I was going to cover up my radiation tattoos.

My oncologist told me to wait six months after my chemo had finished, which happened to be my year anniversary since I was diagnosed. He also said he didn't want it on my right side, where I had my lumpectomy, which I agreed with.

I found a tattoo artist, and for three months, we sent emails back and forth about what I wanted, and I found it helped me leading up to the anniversary. I remember feeling nervous and sad about the whole thing, but getting the tattoo made me feel like I had power, which excited me. It was wild how that worked.

A couple of days before I was supposed to get it, she emailed me to say she had Covid-19. I cried but then thought this has gotten me through the last several months, so I am totally okay with this.

I can't do anything about it. I can handle this, so we just moved it a couple of weeks.

She was amazing. When we were first starting, and I was lying down, she started, and I felt it and started to well up, so she stopped. I explained it felt exactly like when they gave me the radiation tattoo, which I didn't expect. After the shock, I was okay.

Lisa went on to say how having a tattoo made her think deeply about parts of her treatment that affected her.

'I had this feeling, especially in the early stages of being diagnosed, that I didn't know how much longer I would be alive. So I wanted to do something for myself. I didn't want to die without getting a tattoo, and I wanted to experience it before it was too late.

Lisa went on to tell me she was anxious about telling her mother, but like most, she was supportive.

I thought Lisa's uplifting story would be a good place to end my meander through the memories of my cancer treatment.

Ring The Bell

Dear Reader

We are now nearing the end of the book, so let's metaphorically ring the bell. Whatever stage you are at with your cancer treatment, I hope this book has been of use. I know everyone treats you like it's all over, but we all know that the word 'cancer' is always at the back of our minds like an unpaid electricity bill. My advice is don't suffer alone. There is always someone who has experienced what you are feeling and can help.

I know some of the issues I have discussed will traumatise you, and other things will make you laugh. It's a club none of us wants to join, but we are here nonetheless, connected by experience and fear.

Like most things, trauma is best dealt with by talking and, if you can bear it, laughing. With this in mind, my friend Estelle Maher and I have started a podcast called Get it Off Your Chest – The Funny Side of Breast Cancer. If you have any funny breast cancer stories you tell your mates in the pub, we would love to have you on the podcast. You can be outrageous and share your story or be anonymous, and we can tell it for you. Look out for us on all the usual podcast platforms.

Breast reconstruction is still on the cards for me, and I still have some gene results lurking in the background. My pillbox will never be empty, and my body has taken a few knocks, to put it mildly. I am, however, incredibly grateful for the NHS and the support I have received.

I will be back to share more experiences down the road. Thank you for reading this, and good luck to every one of you. Please feel free to get in touch. I would love to hear from you.

Keep going and remember…

stay on the bus!

Love Lolly Pop x

Acknowledgements

The first acknowledgement must go to the University Hospitals of Leicester NHS Trust and its wonderful staff. Not just the incredible consultants and nurses but the cleaners and caterers who made my treatments more bearable. Without the intervention of the NHS, I wouldn't be here today.

Thanks also to the TAUK Publishing team. Their encouragement and expertise helped me to be a finisher for once in my life. This book has opened many doors and allowed me to make friends I wouldn't have met under normal circumstances.

I must also thank the local Loughborough McDonalds and their staff. They filled me with coffee whenever I was manically tapping away, trying to reach another deadline.

Author Bio

Although born in London, Andrea was bought up in rural Suffolk and still loves that part of the world. Now with two kids and a dog, she lives happily in the Midlands.

In April 2018, she was diagnosed with breast cancer and has been through the NHS gold standard treatment, including surgery, chemotherapy and treatment.

While a massive fan of the health system, Andrea found the medical information challenging to read, and that's when the idea for *Stay on the Bus* began to take shape. She hopes it will be a much more palatable read for those undergoing treatment and will help their families and friends understand this difficult time. Her goal is to bring a bit of levity to the experience and hold people's hands through diagnosis and treatment.

Andrea published her first novel, *Throwing Salt at the Devil,* last year and is currently writing a sequel. She is also a co-host of the podcast *Get it Off your Chest: The Funny Side of Breast Cancer.*

She loves hearing from readers and encourages you to follow her on social media to see the alternative side to breast cancer.

Social Media

Instagram: @lollypopstayonthebus & @getitoffyourchestpodcast

Facebook: Andrea Moulding Books & Lolly Pop

Twitter: @BooksMoulding

Podcast: *Get it Off Your Chest: The Funny Side of Breast Cancer* is available on all major podcast platforms.

Glossary

Word	Author Definition
Alka- Seltzer	Sang 'Fizz and the Bits at the Bottom of the Glass' for Austria in the 1978 Eurovision song contest. Does not cure hangovers.
Area 51	Where the conspiracy theorists want to book their two-week vacation.
Avon Lady	For ladies who couldn't be arsed going to the shop for a lipstick and couldn't wait thirty years for the invention of Amazon delivery.
Brewer's Fayre	Where everyone spent their 16th birthday.
Cannulas	One size doesn't fit all. Most people just wish they were as skinny as their veins.
Chemo Brain	When you go out for a pint of milk but come back with a Massey Ferguson tractor MF8700 S.
Cosmopolitan	Full of sex tips which are completely wasted as your undercarriage hasn't seen action since you had your diagnosis.

Word	Author Definition
Dead South	It's not the Island of Wight.
eBay	An expensive car boot sale with sellers that you never get to meet.
Electrical Bug Catcher	The natural progression from duct tape flycatcher that adorns most chippies. Do not buy anything with black bean sauce.
Enthusiastic Nurse	Knows everything about fuck all. While you want to lie in bed, she wants you to sign up for the London marathon with a view to participating in the Olympics—once you feel a bit better.
Faux Leather	Also known as pleather. Feels dead sexy on but gives off a noise only dogs can hear.
Goths	People who struggle in the summer.
Head Honcho	Someone with an elevated sense of importance. Normally wearing Blue Harbour and boat shoes. He smiles a lot when he walks past reception. Always walks past the staff room slowly to see if there are any free cakes.

Word	Author Definition
Intergalactic Ship	For the over fifties, this was the Ford Capri.
Jack Daniels	Usually drank by weathered country singers. Not to be confused with Jack Whitehall, who is a posh boy that hangs around with his dad drinking Bollinger.
Ladies Who Lunch	A pack of hyenas that look like women. Their squeaks can only be by dolphins, whales and bats.
Laboratory Boffins	These people have all been on University Challenge at some point.
Limbo Land	A place that feels a bit like Milton Keynes but has more coffins than roundabouts.
McDonald's	Burgers served with acne.
Misty-eyed	Usually found in most Bette Midler films and cataract wards.
Menopause	Bad thing = hot flushes that could result in you walking around Aldi in your bra. Good thing = also hot flushes, especially with the high fuel prices.

Word	Author Definition
Netflix	For insomniacs, the anti-social, hermits and agoraphobics. Also used in the term 'Netflix and chill'—the universal code for wanna watch Schitt's Creek and have sex.
Newcastle Brown Ale	The drink that Ant and Dec were weaned on.
Outpatient Dept.	Like an airport during Covid where people are draped around the furniture in various states of comatose, drinking vending machine coffee.
Pantomime Villain	Usually slimy, untrustworthy, think their dick is bigger than it actually is. A bit like Nick Hancock.
Parents' Evening	The place where the term 'allotted time' is used a lot but doesn't exist.
Prick	If only it were…
Primark	The shop with a million escalators, where you queue for four days and the bag costs more than the goods you're buying.

Word	Author Definition
Radiohead	More miserable than Morrissey but happier than Chris Martin.
Sinead O'Connor	A wee Irish ting that sang and cried over her Mam or the fact that she looked like she'd just had chemo.
Snogging	Usually practised at the back of youth clubs and the cinema. But the cinema one stopped after 1989 when they built the multiplex and charged £15 a ticket.
Stella Artois Lager	It's French and nasty. A bit like your partner when they have drunk it.
Steptoe	A stage you go through when experiencing initial shock of diagnosis. Symptoms include dirty dishes, furry teeth, matted hair and a full recycle bin.
Students	Usually visit your bedside in groups of four comprising of: the sycophant, the wallflower, the gobshite and the normal one (last one being the only one you hope touches you).

Word	Author Definition
Sunday	2023 sees open churches, shops, cinemas, hospitals, clubs, home delivery. 1973 sees open churches.
Sun-Resistant Clothing	Where style was never a consideration.
Tesco Bag For Life	I mean, how long do you plan on living?
Tiny Tears	Yeah, we all wanted a doll that pissed her knickers!
Toblerone	It only looks nice in the airport, even with the inflated and excessive price tag. You can never break it off one at a time and lots of teeth have been lost to this Swiss confectionery item.
Turmeric	The only thing it can guarantee is staining your dishcloth but has a highly repellent to the properties of bleach.

Word	Author Definition
Woman's Own	Always has the stupid adverts to pay thirty pounds for a carriage clock that you can get for a fiver in Poundland. Also shows you how to fry an egg, the complexities of a fridge and how hot Terry Wogan is even though he's dead.
Valium	The friend you didn't know you needed.

Reference list

[1] Robin Williams discussing Michael Jackson on Propofol, 2011, The Graham Norton Show, Series 10, Episode 5, So Television, Available at: https://www.youtube.com/watch?v=WOIBBE3ObRY [Accessed 14 Jan. 2023].

[2] New blueprint for better hospital food. (2020). [online] gov.uk, Department of Health and Social Care. Available at: https://www.gov.uk/government/news/new-blueprint-for-better-hospital-food.

[3] Smith, C. (2019). Cording a treatable complication of breast cancer surgery. British Journal of General Practice, 69(685): 395.

[4] Szuba A, Rockson SG. Lymphedema: anatomy, physiology and pathogenesis. Vasc. Med. 1997; 2:321Y6. 35.

[5] Pechter, Edward A. M.D., (1998). A New Method for Determining Bra Size and Predicting Postaugmentation Breast Size [online], Volume 102 - Issue 4

[6] Babb, K. (2021). *That's My Size... Or Is It?* [online] Breakout Bras. Available at: https://www.breakoutbras.com/blogs/from-mountains-to-

molehills/thats-my-size [Accessed 21 Jan. 2023].

[7] BBC News. (2019). *A Third of hospitals 'increased Parking charges' Published 10 December 2019 comments*. [online] Available at: https://www.bbc.co.uk/news/health-50718866.

[8] Thorpe-woods, B. (2022). 18 best bathroom cleaning tips. Good housekeeping. [online] 29 Dec. Available at: https://www.goodhousekeeping.com/uk/house-and-home/household-advice/a657043/bathroom-cleaning-tips-sparkling-bathroom/ [Accessed 14 Jan. 2023].

[9] Wikipedia Contributors (2019). Mysophobia. [online] Wikipedia. Available at: https://en.wikipedia.org/wiki/Mysophobia.

[10] Shoemaker, MS, RDN, LD, S. (2019). Published in Healthline.

[11] Jones, B. (2022). *Can You Drink Alcohol During Chemotherapy Treatment?* [online] Verywell Health. Available at: https://www.verywellhealth.com/is-it-safe-to-drink-alcohol-during-chemotherapy-513859.

[12] Casper Blog. (2022). *7 Benefits of Sleeping on Silk Pillowcases | Casper*. [online] Available at: https://casper.com/blog/silk-pillowcase-benefits/ [Accessed 14 Jan. 2023].

[13] Raymaakers, K. (2022). How Can Steroids Help Treat

Cancer? [online] Verywell Health. Available at: https://www.verywellhealth.com/steroids-in-cancer-treatment-2252521.

[14] The Exploress. (2019). *The Exploress podcast.* [online] Available at: https://www.theexploresspodcast.com [Accessed 15 Jan. 2023].

[15] Lawrence, L. (2018). *Easy on the Eyes: Protecting Eye Health Through Cancer Treatments.* [online] Cure Today. Available at: https://www.curetoday.com/view/easy-on-the-eyes-protecting-eye-health-through-cancer-treatments [Accessed 14 Jan. 2023].

[16] Harris V, Hughes M, Roberts R, Dolan G, Williams M, The Development and Testing of a Chemotherapy-Induced Phlebitis Severity (CIPS) Scale for Patients Receiving Anthracycline Chemotherapy for Breast Cancer – J Clin Med. 2020 Mar, 9, 701

[17] Janelsins MC, Kesler SR, Ahles TA, et al. (2014) Prevalence, mechanisms, and management of cancer-related cognitive impairment. International Review of Psychiatry 26(1): 102–113.

[18] Health, uvahealth 10/1/2019 G. (2019). *Dealing With Cancer and Disappearing Friends.* [online] Healthy Balance. Available

at: https://blog.uvahealth.com/2019/10/01/dealing-with-cancer-and-disappearing-friends/ [Accessed 22 Feb. 2023].

[19] Wurtzel, E. (2014). *Prozac Nation*. HarperCollins.

[20] Sharma, A, M.D., Madaan, V, M.D., Petty, FD, M.D., Ph.D., (2006), Prim Care Companion J Clin Psychiatry, Exercise for Mental Health

[21] Lin PJ, Peppone LJ, Janelsins MC, et al. Yoga for the Management of Cancer Treatment-Related Toxicities. Current oncology reports. 2018;20(1):5. [PMC free article] [PubMed] [Google Scholar]

[22] Byram Healthcare. (n.d.). Byram Healthcare. [online] Available at: https://www.byramhealthcare.com/blogs/the-urologic-side-effects-of-breast-cancer-treatment [Accessed 10 Jan. 2023].

[23] Rickett, O. (2020). Britain's desperate lack of public toilets says so much about our country. The Guardian. [online] 27 Jul. Available at: https://www.theguardian.com/commentisfree/2020/jun/27/britain-public-toilets-coronavirus-private-interests.

[24] nhs.uk. (2017). Vaginal dryness. [online] Available at: https://www.nhs.uk/conditions/vaginal-dryness/

[25] Breast Cancer Now. (2017). Genetic testing for altered breast cancer genes. [online] Available at: https://breastcancernow.org/information-support/have-i-got-breast-cancer/family-history/genetic-testing-altered-breast-cancer-genes.

[26] King, S. (2006). Pink Ribbons, Inc. : breast cancer and the politics of philanthropy. Minneapolis, Minn.: University Of Minnesota Press.

[27] Agarwal T, Hultman CS. Impact of radiotherapy and chemotherapy on planning and outcome of breast reconstruction. Breast Disease. 2002;16:37–42. DOI: 10.3233/BD-2002-16107

[28] Lubitz, R. (n.d.). Cancer Took My Breasts—My Mastectomy Tattoo Helped Me Reclaim Them. [online] www.refinery29.com. Available at: https://www.refinery29.com/en-gb/2019/10/8606764/breast-cancer-survivor-mastectomy-tattoo.

Helpful links

This resource list only scratches the surface. If you find something excellent, please share it with me on social media so we can spread the word. This section is organised with the major charities first as they have numerous resources and are worth a deep dive into their websites:

UK Charities

You will likely be familiar with the following UK charities. They offer a wealth of information and support.

Macmillan has many publications and booklets and offers confidential support.

https://www.macmillan.org.uk/cancer-information-and-support/get-help/macmillan-support-line

Cancer Research offers a myriad of booklets and support for breast cancer.

https://www.cancerresearchuk.org/about-cancer/breast-cancer/living-with/resources-books

Breast Cancer Now offers publications and information.

https://breastcancernow.org/

Breast Cancer UK

https://www.breastcanceruk.org.uk/

Maggie's offers free to cancer patients and their families at their centres. They also offer support online.

https://www.maggies.org/

Coppafeel

https://coppafeel.org/

Know Your Lemons

https://www.knowyourlemons.org/

Look Good Feel Better offers courses in makeup and skincare in classes or online.

lookgoodfeelbetter.co.uk/support/women/

Cancer Hair Care- A leading hair loss support charity

https://www.cancerhaircare.co.uk/

DIY Hair Coverings

There are plenty of resources on YouTube. Here are just a few:

How to tie a headscarf during chemotherapy alopecia cancerwithasmile. [online]
https://www.youtube.com/watch?v=tRL2cWklcYg

Fan Wrap with A Tail! Wrapunzel Tutorial! [online]
https://www.youtube.com/watch?v=qskBWHigMGI

How to tie a head scarf for cancer patients. [online]
https://www.youtube.com/watch?v=2K_x6nbOHlU

Telling the children about a breast cancer diagnosis

Depending on the age of your children, there are several resources you will find helpful:

YouTube

Mom Has Cancer: What Comes Next- Talking to Kids About a Family Diagnosis

https://youtu.be/5DTYSnvmecA

London Cancer -Telling your child you have cancer.

https://youtu.be/czzAicecxiQ

Books

There are several books available. Here are just two.

Nowhere Hair: Explains your cancer and chemo to your kids by Sue Glader (Author)

Paperback – 2 May 2013

Cancer Party!: Explain Cancer, Chemo, and Radiation to Kids in a Totally Non-Scary Way by Sara S Olsher (Author) Paperback – 13 Feb 2019

Also, check out Elke Barber, a TED speaker who advocates how to tell children bad news. She was widowed at a young age and is also a breast cancer survivor.

Is Daddy Coming Back in a Minute? Explaining (sudden) death in words very young children can understand by Elke Barber (Author), Alex Barber (Author), Anna Jarvis (Illustrator)

Many of the charities listed above also have information on how to tell children about your diagnosis.

Information on breast cancer and fertility

Podcast

And Then Came Breast Cancer - A Future Dreams Podcast (dated 2 Aug 2021)

You can also find information on the major cancer websites:

Preserving fertility and breast cancer - Cancer Research UK

Cancer and fertility - Macmillan booklet

Cancer and fertility in women - Macmillan Booklet

Bizarre resources that make you laugh

Hubby, B. (n.d.). *Thanks for the Mammories* - hubbyco.com

30 Times Hospital Food Was So Bad, People Just Had to Shame It - https://www.boredpanda.com/

Cosmopolitan article- *A definitive ranking of all the weird (and funny) words for vagina*

https://www.cosmopolitan.com/uk/body/a35357/words-for-vagina/

How to make false boobs

DIY Marta - How to Make Fake Breast Augmentation

https://www.diymarta.com/how-make-fake-breast-augmentation/

Toilet Map

It lets you know where public loos are to relieve the anxiety of being caught short.

toiletmap.org.uk

Tattoos

Nip Charity who have a map of tattoo artists who specialise in mastectomy/breast cancer tattoos

nipcharity.org/artist-directory

How to recycle your medication for those who need it

intercare.org.uk

Information on aesthetic flat closure

notputtingonashirt.org

Exercise

There is a plethora of videos and resources out there. Here is just a taster. Don't rely on Google. Check with a medical team to avoid injury.

Moving Through Cancer

Schmitz, K. (2021). *Moving Through Cancer: An Exercise and Strength-Training Program for the Fight of Your Life empowers Patients and Caregivers in 5 Steps*. Chronicle Prism

movingthroughcancer.com

Kaelin, C., Coltrera, F., Gardiner, J. and Prouty, J. (2007). *The Breast Cancer Survivor's Fitness Plan*. McGraw Hill Professional.

Aaronson, N. and Marie, A. (2014). *Pilates for Breast Cancer Survivors*. Demos Medical Publishing.

Osteoporosis

Facebook Groups

Osteoporosis Education and Support

Osteoporosis Support (UK ONLY)

Osteoporosis UK

Osteoporosis and osteopenia

And finally, an unashamed plug for our podcast:

Get it Off Your Chest: The Funny Side of Breast Cancer podcast – available on all platforms.

Please get in touch if you have any hilarious stories.

Printed in Great Britain
by Amazon

62066633R00151